TRAINING Grundwissen

ENGLISCH

W0379782

Harald Fischer

Englisch 8. Klasse

Aufgaben mit Lösungen

STARK

ISBN: 3-89449-321-6

2. neu bearbeitete und ergänzte Auflage 2004
D-85318 Freising · Postfach 1852 · Tel. (08161) 1790

Inhalt

(Fortsetzung siehe nächste Seite)

Autor: Harald Fischer
Illustrator: Igor Schulz-Bertram

Vorwort

Liebe Schülerin, lieber Schüler,

den ersten Schritt auf dem Weg zu besseren Leistungen im Fach Englisch hast du bereits getan: Toll, dass du bereit bist, mit diesem Trainingsbuch zu arbeiten! Es wird dir helfen, den Englischstoff der 8. Klasse besser zu bewältigen.

- Der Unterrichtsstoff wird mit kurzen **Erklärungen** und vielen anschaulichen **Beispielen** erläutert.
- Dann folgen abwechslungsreiche **Übungen**, die häufig auf Bildern aufbauen. Der Schwierigkeitsgrad steigert sich dabei kontinuierlich; besonders schwierige Aufgaben sind mit einem ✸ versehen.
- Über die verschiedenen Kapitel sind **Tipps und Übungen für das Verfassen eigener Texte** verteilt. Sie geben dir wichtige Informationen darüber, was zu beachten ist, wenn du z. B. ein Interview, einen Dialog oder eine Bildbeschreibung anfertigen möchtest.
- Am Ende des Buches kannst du anhand der **Lösungen** kontrollieren, ob du alles richtig verstanden hast.
- Falls du ein Wort nicht kennst: Kein Problem, denn du kannst es im Kapitel **Schwierige Wörter** nachschlagen.

Du kannst mit diesem Trainingsbuch ganz individuell lernen, so wie du es brauchst. Das Buch muss nicht von Anfang bis Ende durchgearbeitet werden, du kannst auch einfach im Inhaltsverzeichnis das für dich gerade wichtige Kapitel heraussuchen. Allerdings solltest du ein Kapitel von Anfang an durchgehen, weil du dabei wichtiges Grundwissen nochmals auffrischst.

Und nun viel Spaß und Erfolg beim Üben!

Harald Fischer

… rund ums Nomen

1 Bestimmte und unbestimmte Artikel

Nomen werden häufig zusammen mit einem **Begleiter** gebraucht. Einer dieser Begleiter ist der **Artikel**. Sowohl den bestimmten Artikel *(the)* als auch den unbestimmten *(a, an)* kannst du in den meisten Fällen genauso benutzen wie im Deutschen.

Rund um bestimmte Artikel

Wann verwendest du den bestimmten Artikel?

Im Allgemeinen stellst du den **bestimmten Artikel** *(definite article)* einem Nomen voran, wenn von einer **ganz bestimmten Person oder Sache** die Rede ist und nicht von irgendeiner beliebigen.

Beispiele: The teacher said, "Give me the sponge, please!"

Mit bestimmtem Artikel

- Familiennamen im Plural, Namen mit *of*, geografische Namen (z. B. Ländernamen im Plural, Gebirge, Sehenswürdigkeiten, Flüsse, Meere)

  Beispiele:
  The Harrisons are here today.
  You must see the Tower of London.
  Many tourists from the USA spend their holidays in the Alps.
  The Golden Gate Bridge is San Francisco's landmark.
  The Thames flows into the North Sea.

- Gebäudebezeichnungen, Institutionen, Verkehrsmittel, wenn ein ganz bestimmtes Gebäude, Fahrzeug etc. gemeint ist

  Beispiele:
  This is the High School I attend.
  Where is the prison in your town?
  Is this the bus to Dulwich?

Ohne bestimmtem Artikel

- Namen von Personen im Singular, Ländernamen im Singular, Namen von einzelnen Bergen, Seen, Straßen

  Beispiele:
  Did you see Peter?
  When you are in Scotland, go and climb Ben Nevis!
  Lake Windermere is the nicest lake I know.
  Our school is in Lincoln Street.

- Gebäudebezeichnungen, Institutionen, Verkehrsmittel, wenn der Verwendungszweck im Vordergrund steht

  Beispiele:
  We go to school every day.
  They sent him to prison.
  Why do you always go by bus?

- abstrakte Begriffe, Stoffbezeichnungen, zählbare Nomen im Plural, Zeitbestimmungen, wenn sie näher bestimmt werden

Beispiele:
I hate the noise of school children.
This is the graphite they use for pencils.
The pencils on my desk must be sharpened.
You remember the holidays we spent in Texas?

- abstrakte Begriffe, Stoffbezeichnungen, zählbare Nomen im Plural, Zeitbestimmungen, wenn sie allgemein verwendet werden

Beispiele:
Noise is something terrible.
Graphite is used for making pencils.
All pupils like holidays.

Aufgabe 1 Translate into English.

a) Sandy ist auf dem Weg in die Schule. Sie denkt: „Hoffentlich treffe ich heute Lisa.“

____

____

b) In der Breiten Straße trifft sie tatsächlich ihre Freundin, die ihre Ferien am Lake Michigan verbracht hat.

____

____

c) Lisa sagt, dass sie auch in New York war und dort das Empire State Building, den East River und den Broadway gesehen hat.

____

____

Aufgabe 2 Definite Article – yes or no?

Last year, Mr Brown, our history teacher, had to stay in ________[1] hospital for six weeks. We visited him once in ______[2] hospital in ________[3] Glenn Close. Of course, we had ______[4] lessons with our headteacher. We don't like her, and ______[5] lessons she gives are really bad; so we were very glad when Mr Brown finally came back ______[6] week before ______[7] Christmas holidays. With him, ______[8] history is really fun!

We talked a lot about _____[9] ancient times, especially about _____[10] time of the Roman Empire, and about ________[11] war and ________[12] peace. We heard that _____[13] wars fought by the Roman Emperors were quite terrible. One of _____[14] lessons was absolutely fantastic.

When one of my classmates, ______[15] Mark, asked Mr Brown if he could show us ______[16] pictures of ________[17] Roman castles, he took a book out of his desk and showed us a few of ______[18] castles the Romans built in ______[19] country that is now ______[20] Germany.

______[21] following week, we talked about ______[22] history of ______[23] United States. We heard about ______[24] War of ______[25] Independence, ______[26] Civil War, ______[27] slavery and ______[28] Prohibition. On __________[29] map, Mr Brown showed us __________[30] Gettysburg, where Lincoln spoke, and __________[31] San Antonio, where Davy Crockett saved Texas in ______[32] battle of ______[33] Alamo.

Rund um unbestimmte Artikel

Wann verwendest du den unbestimmten Artikel?

Im Allgemeinen steht vor einem Nomen der **unbestimmte Artikel** *(indefinite article)*, wenn eine **nicht näher bestimmte Person oder Sache** genannt wird.

Beispiel: I have an idea!

Mit unbestimmtem Artikel

- Nationalitätenbezeichnungen, Berufsangaben, Religionszugehörigkeit

  Beispiele:
  My teacher is an American.
  I want to become a butler.
  Are you a Catholic?

- nach *half, such, what* sowie nach *as* (deutsch: ‚als')

  Beispiele:
  Half a dozen eggs, please.
  He's such a bore!
  What a pity!
  What did you buy as a souvenir?

- bei Zeit-, Mengen- und Maßangaben (deutsch: ‚pro')

  Beispiele:
  He eats five times a day.
  Sausages cost two pounds a pair.
  Water is forty cents a bottle.

Ohne unbestimmtem Artikel

- Titel, wenn nur eine bestimmte Person in einem Ort, in einer Region etc. den Titel führt

  Beispiel:
  Why do you want to be President of the United States?

Aufgabe 3 Brian's family has a new au pair girl. Wanda, a friend of his, is talking to him about her. Complete Wanda's questions and Brian's answers. Mind the indefinite article!

WANDA: You call your au pair Sam. Isn't that a boy [1]?

BRIAN: No, no, she is really __________ [2]. Her name is Samantha.

WANDA: You say she comes from a reservation. So she is __________ [3]?

BRIAN: Yes, she is __________ [4].

WANDA: And her father works as __________ [5].

BRIAN: But he isn't __________ [6]. Only __________ [7] can be boss!

WANDA: I see. I know the problem. My mother would never accept someone like Sam, she would only want __________ [8]. Is Sam such __________ [9] as our au pair?

BRIAN: Oh yes, she makes brilliant dishes. And what __________ [10] she is; she tells us stories __________ [11].

WANDA: Our au pair brought me a children's book as __________ [12]. Did Sam bring you anything?

BRIAN: Of course she did. She brought earrings for everybody. She had made them herself, but I think in a shop they'd cost ten dollars __________ [13].

WANDA: Great! I think I really must come and see Sam!

Aufgabe 4 Who is who? Mary McMiller has five pen-friends in different countries. The sentences below will help you to find out their names, the cities in which they live, their hobbies and their parents' professions. Complete the sentences with definite or indefinite articles where needed, fill in the table, and answer the questions (n and o).

name	town	hobby	parents' profession

a) _____ museum guide likes to take _____ walk through _____ Hyde Park and around _____ Buckingham Palace.

b) Mary sends all _____ stamps she gets to _____ Sabine.

c) Roy lives near _____ Golden Gate Bridge.

d) Patricia swam _____ 100 metres half _____ second faster this week than last.

e) One of _____ two boys likes _____ air in _____ Rockies when he climbs _____ mountains.

f) Sabine's mother is _____ bus driver, so she can go by _____ bus for free.

g) Riding _____ bike on _____ beach at _____ weekends is _____ fun for Maria and her parents.

h) Mary likes _____ stamps from _____ Luxemburg _____ lot.

i) Thanks to his father, Thomas has free entrance to _____ British Museum.

j) The biker is _____ manageress of _____ Grand Hotel in _____ Rio de Janeiro, and she has a daughter.

k) Sabine isn't _____ American.

l) Mr Spice's daughter often visits him at _____ office of _____ Barclay's Bank on _____ Broadway, where he works as _____ bank clerk.

m) Two of _____ five pen-friends live in _____ USA, so Mary writes four letters _____ month to _____ North America.

n) Who often goes to _____ cinema in London? Answer: _____

o) Where does _____ architect design his houses? Answer: _____

2 Pronomen und Begleiter

Wie du weißt, stehen Nomen im Satz meist zusammen mit einem anderen Wort. Diese Wörter können Artikel *(article)* oder Begleiter *(determiner)* sein. Lediglich Eigennamen stehen ohne Artikel bzw. ohne Begleiter.

Beispiele: The / This / Your } exercise-book is yellow.
Did you see Peter?

Anders als ein Begleiter **ersetzt ein Pronomen *(pronoun)* ein Nomen**. Es wird also vor allem dann gebraucht, wenn man ein Nomen nicht wiederholen will.

Beispiel: Patricia and George came up to me and I said hello to them.

Wenn in einem Satz ein Pronomen benutzt wird, muss das Nomen, an dessen Stelle es steht, **bereits genannt** worden sein oder **als bekannt vorausgesetzt** werden können, d. h. also, dass ein Pronomen nicht anstelle eines erst später eingeführten Nomens stehen kann.

Beispiele: Susan asked me a question, and I couldn't answer Susan.
Susan asked me a question, and I couldn't answer her.

2.1 Personalpronomen

Personalpronomen *(personal pronouns)* stehen stellvertretend für eine Person oder Sache.

Rund um Subjekt- und Objektformen der Personalpronomen

Welche Subjekt- und Objektformen gibt es?

Personalpronomen unterscheiden sich meist in ihrer Form, je nachdem, ob sie als Subjekt oder als Objekt in einem Satz erscheinen.

Person	Subjektform	Objektform
1. Person, Singular	I	me
2. Person, Singular	you	you
3. Person, Singular	he, she, it	him, her, it
1. Person, Plural	we	us
2. Person, Plural	you	you
3. Person, Plural	they	them

- In der 3. Person Singular werden Dinge und Tiere immer durch das Pronomen *it* ersetzt. Für Tiere, denen man einen Namen gegeben hat, kannst du auch *he* oder *she* bzw. *him* oder *her* verwenden.

- Im Englischen gibt es keine Unterschiede zwischen den Formen des direkten und des indirekten Objekts der Personalpronomen.

  Beispiele: Our teacher always gives us a lot of homework.
  (indirektes Objekt)

  When he sees us in the street, he always looks away.
  (direktes Objekt)

- Hat ein Satz zwei Personalpronomen in der Objektform, so steht das indirekte zuerst oder es wird mit *to* hinter das direkte gestellt.

  Beispiel: We must show our teacher our homework.
  We must show him it. **oder** We must show it to him.

- Auch **nach Präpositionen** und **in betonter Stellung** musst du die Personalpronomen der **Objektform** verwenden.

  Beispiele: He never talks to us outside the classroom.
  Who do you mean? Him?

Aufgabe 1 Mike's bike is gone (I): Put in the subject and object forms of the pronouns.

When he came out of the school building last Thursday, Mike couldn't find his bike.

"Hey, am ________[1] dreaming? Where's my bike? ________[2]'s gone. I can't see ________[3] anywhere!" Suddenly Mike saw Petula, and ________[4] asked ________[5]: "Hey Petula, do ________[6] know where my bike is? Come on, tell ________[7]!" ________[8] answered: "Don't ask ________[9]! I didn't see ________[10] when you arrived this morning! Look, Kalvin and Conny are coming. ______[11]'m sure ________[12] can tell ________[13]!"

"I don't want to ask ________[14]. ________[15] aren't friends, you know!" But Kalvin and Conny had already heard, so ______[16] asked: "What don't ______[17] want to ask ________[18]? Come on, perhaps we can help ________[19]!" So Mike had to tell ________[20] about his bike, but they couldn't help ________[21] either. In the end, ________[22] could only do one thing: go to the police.

Aufgabe 2 The German pronoun 'sie' has several different meanings. So be careful when you translate the following sentences.

a) Ist das deine Schultasche? Sie ist sehr schön. Darf ich sie nehmen?

____

b) Wo sind Peter und Francis? Siehst du sie? Ach, da sind sie ja!

____

c) Gehen Sie oft hier spazieren? Ich habe Sie noch nie gesehen.

____

d) Darf ich vorstellen? Das ist Cecilia. Du hast sie noch nicht getroffen; sie ist meine Cousine aus Kanada.

____

____

Rund um Possessivpronomen und -begleiter

Wann verwendest du Possessivpronomen und Possessivbegleiter?

Possessivpronomen (*possessive pronouns*) und Possessivbegleiter (*possessive determiners*) beschreiben ein **Besitzverhältnis** oder – allgemeiner gefasst – eine **Zugehörigkeit** bzw. **Verbundenheit**.

Possessivbegleiter stehen immer vor dem zugehörigen Nomen. Possessivpronomen verwendest du dann, wenn du ein Nomen und seinen Possessivbegleiter durch ein einziges Wort ersetzen möchtest. Possessivpronomen stehen immer ohne Nomen.

Beispiel: This is <u>your book</u>. → It is <u>yours</u>.

Welche Possessivpronomen und -begleiter gibt es?

Die Possessivpronomen und -begleiter musst du auswendig lernen.

Personalpronomen		Possessivbegleiter		Possessivpronomen
I	→	my	→	mine
you	→	your	→	yours
he	→	his	→	his
she	→	her	→	hers
it	→	its	→	its
we	→	our	→	ours
you	→	your	→	yours
they	→	their	→	theirs

Aufgabe 3 The German word 'ihr(e)' has several different meanings. So be careful when you translate the following sentences.

a) Ist Ihr Klassenzimmer im ersten Stock, Frau Price?

____

b) Meine Kinder machen gerade ihre Hausaufgaben.

____

c) Gib diesen Taschenrechner bitte meiner Schwester; es ist ihrer. Du kannst ihr sagen, dass ich ihr ihr Buch morgen geben werde.

____

____

d) Ihr könnt doch nicht einfach so das Klassenzimmer verlassen!

____

e) Die Turnhalle und die Treppe, die zu ihr führt, sind heute sehr schmutzig, aber meistens ist unsere Schule und ihre Umgebung völlig sauber.

____

____

Aufgabe 4 Mike's bike is gone (II): Put in possessive pronouns and possessive determiners.

Mr Smart, a police officer, has found some stolen bikes in Robby Rob's garage and invites Mike and other people to have a look at them.

MR SMART: Well now, Mike, is any of these bikes _____ [1]?

MIKE: I'm not sure. This one looks like _____ [2] bike, but _____ [3] had smaller handlebars. These look like Betty's; perhaps they're _____ [4].

MR SMART: You're right, _____ [5] bike is gone, too. But she said _____ [6] frame was red, not yellow. Weren't your bikes yellow, Mr and Mrs White?

MRS WHITE: Yes, _____ [7] were yellow, but they were much bigger. _____ [8] bikes were very expensive ones, and _____ [9] saddles were black, not grey!

MR WHITE: That's true. You know, my wife always buys top quality, so _____ [10] was really the best bike in our street!

MR SMART: I see. And I suppose _____ [11] was second best, wasn't it?

MIKE: Hey, Mrs White, couldn't this be _____ [12] bike? And that one Mr White's?

MR SMART: No, Mike, I think _____ [13] are over there, and this one is _____ [14].

Rund um Reflexivpronomen und reziproke Pronomen

Wann verwendest du Reflexivpronomen?

- Du verwendest Reflexivpronomen (*reflexive pronouns*) dann, wenn **Subjekt und Objekt** eines Satzes **dieselbe Person bezeichnen**.

  Beispiel: When he saw himself in the mirror, he laughed.

- Reflexivpronomen kannst du auch **zur Hervorhebung eines Nomens oder Pronomens** verwenden. Im Deutschen wird dieses Reflexivpronomen häufig durch Verstärker wie ‚selbst', ‚höchstpersönlich' wiedergegeben.

  Beispiel: Sarah and Judy really did their homework themselves!

- Reflexive Verben sind im Deutschen viel zahlreicher als im Englischen, daher Vorsicht beim Übersetzen!

Beispiele:	to care about	sich kümmern um
	to change	sich ändern/sich umziehen
	to differ	sich unterscheiden
	to fall in love	sich verlieben
	to happen	sich ereignen
	to imagine	sich vorstellen
	to recover	sich erholen
	to rely on	sich verlassen auf
	to remember	sich erinnern
	to rise	sich erheben
	to settle	sich niederlassen
	to sit down	sich hinsetzen

Welche Reflexivpronomen gibt es?

Auch die Reflexivpronomen musst du auswendig lernen.

Personalpronomen		**Reflexivpronomen**
I	→	myself
you	→	yourself
he, she, it	→	himself, herself, itself
we	→	ourselves
you	→	yourselves
they	→	themselves

Aufgabe 5 Translate.

Viele deutsche Schüler können sich nicht vorstellen, dass sich englische Schulen von deutschen deutlich (widely) unterscheiden. Nur wer sich für längere Zeit an einer Schule in England befindet, wird sich dort auch wohlfühlen können. In jedem Falle wird er sich noch lange an all das erinnern können, was in England anders ist. Zum Beispiel erheben sich Schüler in manchen Schulen, wenn der Lehrer das Klassenzimmer betritt, und morgens ist es der Schulleiter persönlich, der die Schüler begrüßt.

___

___

___

___

___

Wann verwendest du reziproke Pronomen?

Reflexivpronomen werden, wie du eben gesehen hast, dann verwendet, wenn ausgedrückt werden soll, dass eine Person oder eine Gruppe von Personen etwas in Bezug auf sich selbst tut. Hingegen verwendest du die **reziproken Pronomen** *(reciprocal pronouns) each other* und *one another* dann, wenn du eine **wechselseitige Beziehung** ausdrücken willst.

Beispiel: The pupils in the class usually know each other well.

Aufgabe 6 Choose a verb from the list to describe what you see in the pictures. Make sentences with reflexive and reciprocal pronouns.
buy, write, clean, teach, look, help

a) 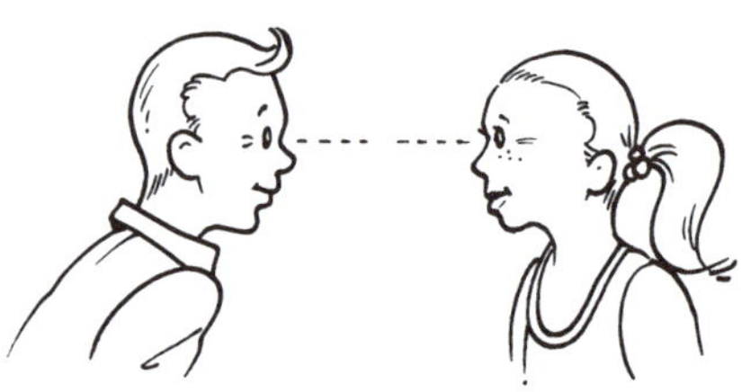

Toby and Charlotte are

___

b)

The cat ______________________
____

c)

Mr and Mrs Rice ______________
____

d)

Alina and Willy ______________
____

e)

Denise ______________________
____

f)

Pat and Mike _________________
____

Tipps zum Schreiben eines Interviews

In einem Interview geht es hauptsächlich um Fragen und Antworten auf diese Fragen – also um Inhalte. Darüber hinaus solltest du aber versuchen, das Interview **so lebendig und echt wie möglich** zu gestalten. Ein Interview lässt sich in drei Teile einteilen:

Teil A: Begrüßung, Vorstellung des Themas
- Am Anfang begrüßen sich die Interviewpartner.
- Dann erklärt der Interviewer, wozu das Interview dienen soll.

Teil B: Hauptteil mit Fragen und Antworten
- Der Interviewer muss mindestens drei Fragen parat haben.
- Der Befragte darf Gegenfragen stellen.
- Der Befragte darf erwähnen, dass der Interviewer das soeben Gesagte sicher schon weiß.
- Der Interviewer darf sagen, was er zum Thema weiß, und daran Fragen anschließen.
- Eine Antwort darf auch einmal ungenau sein; der Interviewer kann dann nachfragen.

Teil C: Verabschiedung
Am Ende bedanken und verabschieden sich die Interviewpartner.

Verwende **ganz normales Englisch**, vergiss aber nicht, **Fachausdrücke** einzubauen, soweit das möglich oder nötig ist. Die Interviewpartner sprechen miteinander. Dein Interview sollte daher die **Besonderheiten des gesprochenen Englisch** aufweisen, wie z. B. Kurzformen (z. B. *can't*, won't), Füllwörter (z. B. *well, you know*), Ausrufe (z. B. *Oh dear! Oh no!*), *question tags* (z. B. *…, isn't it?*) und nicht allzu lange Sätze.

Aufgabe 7* Here is some information about British schools:

- British pupils have to wear school uniform
- in many schools, classes start at 9 a.m.
- in many schools, lessons are 50 minutes
- there is a lunch break of about one hour
- most schools have a school cafeteria where pupils can get warm meals
- there are classes in the afternoon
- primary school is from age 5 to 11
- from year 7, most pupils go to comprehensive schools
- pupils take their A-levels at age 18 after "sixth form"
- as an alternative to state-run schools, public (fee-paying) schools accept pupils from age 13 to 18

Dorothy, a 14-year-old girl from Newcastle, is visiting your school as an exchange student. Your friends from your school magazine have asked you to interview her and find out about differences between the German and the British school system. Write the interview.

2.2 Unbestimmte Pronomen und Begleiter

Zu den unbestimmten Pronomen und Begleitern *(indefinite pronouns and determiners)* gehören Wörter wie *some, many, any, none.* Mit ihnen kann man Mengen beschreiben, ohne dabei genaue Angaben zu machen.

Rund um *some* und *any*

Wann benutzt du *some* und *any*?

Du gebrauchst *some* und *any* bei **nicht zählbaren Nomen** und bei den **Pluralformen von Nomen**.

Beispiele: I need some water.
Some pupils are cleverer than others.

Außerdem gelten die folgenden Regeln:

- Du benutzt *some* nur in **bejahten Sätzen** und in **Fragen**, auf die du als **Antwort ‚ja'** erwartest.

  Beispiele: I need some chalk, please.
  Could you fetch me some, please?

- Du benutzt *any* in **verneinten Sätzen** und in **Fragen**.

  Beispiele: There isn't any chalk left.
  Do you need any help?

- Bei der **Übersetzung ins Deutsche** bleiben *some* und *any* oftmals **unübersetzt**.

  Beispiel: Are there any chairs?
  Sind Stühle da?

- Für die **Zusammensetzungen** von *some* und *any (compounds)*, also für *somebody, someone, something, somewhere, somehow, anybody, anyone, anything, anywhere, anyhow,* gelten die **gleichen Regeln**.

  Beispiel: Could somebody come to the blackboard, please?

Aufgabe 8 The lost pencil-case. Put in some or any, or one of their compounds.

JANE: Has ______________ [1] found my pencil-case at last?

ANN: No, we can't see it ____________________ [2].

JANE: But it must be _________________ [3]. I didn't see ______________ [4] taking it outside!

BOB: Perhaps ______________ [5] has put it in his or her school-bag!

CARL: But we all haven't, and there haven't been ______________ [6] other pupils in the room since Jane lost it.

JANE: Perhaps _______________ [7] of you saw what I did with it?

BOB: Oh no, sorry, but _____________________ [8] we don't look at you but at ______________ [9] else! Still, I'm sure we'll find it ______________ [10].

ANN: What about that chair over there? Has ______________________ [11] looked there?

JANE: Oh dear, I can't believe it, we've found it. _____________________ [12] idiot must have put it there! Thank you, all of you!

Rund um *every, each, any, all*

Wann benutzt du *every, each, any* und *all?*

each und *all* sowie *every* und *any* und ihre Zusammensetzungen gebrauchst du vor Nomen im Sinne des deutschen Wortes ‚jeder'.

- *every* bedeutet: jeder, im allgemeinen Sinne

  Beispiel: We get up early every day.
- *each* bedeutet: jeder einzelne

  Beispiel: I loved each day of our summer holidays.
- *any* bedeutet: jeder beliebige

  Beispiel: You can come any day.
- *all* bedeutet: alle, ohne Ausnahme

  Beispiel: All my holidays this year were great.

Vorsicht mit dem deutschen Wort ‚alle':

Beispiele:	All children must go to school.	(uneingeschränkt alle)
	All the pupils in our class are right-handed.	(alle in einer bestimmten Gruppe)
	Everybody can do that.	(‚alle' ohne Nomen)

Aufgabe 9 Put in suitable forms of *every, each, any, anything* and *all.*

In the gymnasium, the P.E. teacher is talking to her pupils.
"I know that you are ____________________ [1] interested in sports, but I know too that ____________________ [2] pupil likes different kinds of sport. Unfortunately, we can't do ____________________ [3] here, and I'm not ready to play ____________________ [4] game with you, but perhaps we can play a different game in ____________________ [5] lesson. This means that ____________________ [6] of you must tell me what she likes, and I will try to remember ____________________ [7] your answers. You can say ____________________ [8] you like, but you must make sure that ____________________ [9] the pupils are able to do it. Has ____________________ [10] of you understood?"

Rund um *a lot of, many, much, (a) few, (a) little*

Wann benutzt du *a lot of, many, much, (a) few, (a) little?*

Bei den unbestimmten Pronomen *a lot of, many, much, (a) few, (a) little* musst du unterscheiden, ob von zählbaren oder nicht zählbaren Begriffen die Rede ist.

im Sinne von	zählbar	nicht zählbar
viele, viel	many desks / a lot of desks	much luck / a lot of luck
ein paar, etwas	a few desks	a little luck
wenige, wenig	few desks	little luck
weniger	fewer desks	less luck

Aufgabe 10 Why do they all like holidays? Put in *a lot of, many, much, (a) few, (a) little.*

There's not ________ [1] work to do.

There's ________ [2] time for fun.

There are ________ [3] happy hours.

There are ________ [4] discussions about school.

There's ________ [5] fear of school.

There are only ________ [6] boring days (if at all).

There are ________ [7] visitors.

There's ________ [8] happiness.

There's ________ [9] to learn.

Rund um *no, none*

Wann benutzt du *no, none?*

- *no* im Sinne von ‚kein' steht wie ein Adjektiv immer vor einem Nomen.

  Beispiel: We have no school today.

- *none* (‚keiner') gebrauchst du, wenn du das Nomen nicht wiederholen willst, oder vor einer *of*-Gruppe.

  Beispiele: How many brothers and sisters have you got? – None.
  None of my brothers and sisters really hates school.

ıfgabe 11 Mike's bike is gone (III): Put in indefinite pronouns and determiners.

In Robby Rob's house, the police have found lots of other stolen things. A police spokesman, Mr Loudly, is showing them to journalists.

MR LOUDLY: Well, ladies and gentlemen, here you can see ____________[1] we found in Mr Rob's house. It's ____________[2], isn't it?

TV REPORTER: Yes, it is, but why are you showing us so ____________[3] bikes? You said you had found ____________[4] more.

MR LOUDLY: That's easy. We have already given ____________[5] of them to their owners, so there are ____________[6] left than you probably expected to see.

NEWSPAPERMAN: Could you please give us ____________[7] information on how you found Mr Rob? You have told us very ____________[8] so far.

MR LOUDLY: I'm afraid I can't tell you ____________[9] now; it's all secret!

NEWSPAPERMAN: But ____________[10] must be allowed to tell us ____________[11] things! You have had so ____________[12] success already, so you can tell us ____________[13] more!

MR LOUDLY: You will hear ____________[14] from me, and the police constables here know even ____________[15] than I do, so don't ask them! ____________[16] of us will help you.

TV REPORTER: But we must find out ____________[17]. That's our job!

MR LOUDLY: I'm sorry. ____________[18] policeman will ever give away secrets! Goodbye!

Rund um *either, neither, both*

Wann benutzt du *either, neither, both*?

- *either* verwendest du in der Bedeutung ‚jeder von beiden', ‚der eine oder der andere'.
  Beispiel: Either (of them) likes history.
- *neither* verwendest du dementsprechend in der Bedeutung ‚keiner von beiden'.
  Beispiel: Neither of my parents is at home when I come back from school.
- *either* und *neither* sind Bestandteile einer ganzen Reihe von Ausdrücken:

‚auch nicht'	not either
‚weder … noch …'	neither … nor …
‚Ich auch nicht.'	Neither do/can/have/must I.
‚Ich auch.'	So do I.
‚Ich schon.'	I do, though.

- *both* bedeutet ‚alle beide'. Es steht meist vor dem Nomen. Das Nomen kann aber auch mit *of* angeschlossen werden.
  Beispiele: Both schools are good.
  Both of my neighbours are better than I am.

Aufgabe 12* A strange story. Turn the text into a good story by rewriting the underlined parts, using indefinite pronouns, indefinite determiners, reflexive pronouns and reflexive verbs.

One day last October, I met my friend Carol at the school cafeteria. She was accompanied by her cousin, who was new at our school. I didn't know the girl, and she didn't know me, so I told her my name, and Chris told me hers.
We all took a seat in a corner. I looked around, and Carol looked around, too. "What are we going to have?" Carol asked. I looked at Chris, and she looked at me, and we said at the same time, "Sausages and mashed potatoes." Now, I know that Carol is very lazy, but – believe it or not! – Carol – not Chris nor me – stood up and went to the counter. She got bacon and eggs for Chris and for herself and brought everything to our table. Chris said, "I don't really like lunch at the cafeteria." I answered, "It's the same with me". But Carol said, "I don't agree!" Carol added that there were always two meals to choose from, and she always liked the first and the second meal. Chris looked at me, but she didn't answer, and I didn't answer. After lunch, it came to my mind again that I had agreed to meet Laury before the end of lunch-time, so I said good-bye to the two girls. "Sorry, but I have to go quickly. I'm glad that I saw you and you saw me. See you again soon!"

gabe 13* Complete the story with pronouns and determiners, and write the words into the squares according to the numbers given in brackets. Each word starts with the last letter of the word before. The grey squares will give you the letters for the last word.

Last Wednesday, Mr Little, our English teacher, came into the classroom and said to (12) ____________: "Today, I've got a riddle for (11) __________. You must find something; it's not a thing, but I wish (4) ____________ of it to (5) ____________ of you. Let's see if you can find out (15) __________."
"Can (2) __________ have it?", asked Linda, and (1) __________ added, "And can I give it to Jim?" "Well," answered Mr Little, "you can't give it to (6) ___________, but it will be (3) ___________ if you work hard." "Why can it be (9) __________ and not (7) ___________?" cried Jim, who had misunderstood Mr Little. "Oh, Jim, you can get it, but when (10) __________ else has it, he can't pass it on. By the way, he can't throw it away, (17) ___________."
"Okay," I said at last, "let's see what (16) ___________ have got. It can be (14) __________ but people can't pass it on to (8) ____________ other. We'd like to have it, and (13) ____________ would Mr Little. That really isn't much. I think we give up!"
"That's a pity!" said Mr Little. "All right, here's the solution: I wish you a lot of ..."

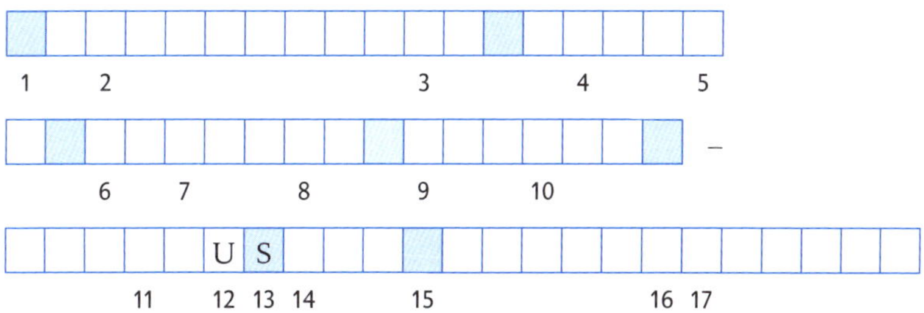

__ __ __ __ __ __ __

3 Adjektive

Adjektive (*adjectives*) sind Wörter wie *small, several, yellow, nice.* Mit ihnen kann man die **Eigenschaften** oder **Merkmale von Lebewesen, Dingen, Begriffen** und **Zuständen näher beschreiben.**

3.1 Einsatzmöglichkeiten von Adjektiven

An welche Stelle im Satz stellst du ein Adjektiv?

Ein **Adjektiv** kann **vor dem zugehörigen Nomen** stehen (attributiver Gebrauch) oder **nach bestimmten Verben** – vor allem nach *be* (prädikativer Gebrauch).

Beispiele: I know a lot of interesting places in New York. (attributiv)
But some of them are dangerous. (prädikativ)

Aufgabe 1 12 adjectives and their opposites are hidden in the letter field on page 24. They can be written in any direction, forwards and backwards. The opposite of the 25th adjective is not in the letter field; you can make it from the seven letters which do not belong to any adjective.

_______________ _______________
_______________ _______________
_______________ _______________
_______________ _______________
_______________ _______________
_______________ _______________
_______________ _______________
_______________ _______________
_______________ _______________
_______________ _______________
_______________ _______________
_______________ _______________
_______________ _______________

D	L	B	F	H	G	I	H	U	D	L
I	N	T	E	R	E	S	T	I	N	G
F	D	S	D	A	L	G	F	F	N	S
F	A	Y	L	G	U	F	A	I	I	L
E	S	S	R	I	I	T	R	M	D	O
R	W	A	T	C	M	O	I	I	L	W
E	E	E	U	K	B	L	T	F	O	S
N	N	L	H	E	A	V	Y	L	U	S
T	T	H	A	R	D	T	H	G	I	L

Aufgabe 2 Say why Ben is so unhappy, and Betty is so happy. Use some of the adjectives from exercise 1.

Ben doesn't like sports, because he is ____________ 1 and too ____________ 2. In his room he has an ____________ 3 poster and an ____________ 4 computer with a very ____________ 5 game. He always gets ____________ 6 homework, and he is a ____________ 7 worker, so he rarely meets his friends, who live ____________ 8 away, anyway.

Betty likes sports, because she is ____________ 9 and ____________ 10. In her room, she has a ____________ 11 poster and a ____________ 12 computer with a very ____________ 13 game. The homework she gets is always ____________ 14 and she is a ____________ 15 worker, so she has a lot of time to meet her friends, who live ____________ 16 her house.

Wie im Deutschen werden Adjektive auch in **nominaler Form** (meist zusammen mit dem bestimmten Artikel) verwendet. Sie bezeichnen eine **Gruppe von Menschen oder Dingen**, auf die die entsprechende Eigenschaft zutrifft. Die Adjektive werden dann wie Pluralformen verwendet, haben aber kein Plural-s. Wenn einzelne Personen gemeint sind, so musst du das Adjektiv durch ein Nomen ergänzen, was dann wieder dem attributiven Gebrauch entspricht.

Beispiele: In New York, <u>the rich</u> and <u>the poor</u> live very close to each other.
<u>This poor man</u> needs help.

Ebenso kannst du in einigen Fällen ein Volk bezeichnen, ohne das Adjektiv in den Plural zu setzen.

Beispiel: <u>The English</u> are always shocked when they see that.

Aufgabe 3 Complete the following proverbs with suitable adjectives.

a) Better ________________ than never.

b) One law for the ____________ and another for the ______________.

c) Ask a _____________ question and you get a ______________ answer.

d) The ________________ die young.

e) Strike while the iron is __________________.

f) A __________________ key can open any door.

g) Never speak ill of the __________________.

h) The ______________________ are a nation of shop-keepers.

i) __________________ habits die hard.

j) __________________ sacks will never stand upright.

k) He who laughs last, laughs _________________.

l) Hope for the ______________ and prepare for the ______________.

m) All's for the _____________ in the ___________ of all possible worlds.

n) The grass is always _______________ on the other side of the fence.

o) ______________ things ______________.

3.2 Steigerung von Adjektiven und Vergleiche

Wann steigerst du Adjektive?

Steigerungsformen verwendest du dann, wenn du verschiedene **Abstufungen von Eigenschaften** ausdrücken willst.

Beispiel: New York is an old city. (Positiv)
London is older. (Komparativ)
London is the oldest city in England. (Superlativ)

Wann verwendest du Vergleiche?

Du gebrauchst **Vergleiche**, wenn du **Gleichheit** oder **Ungleichheit** beschreiben willst.

Beispiel: I think London is nicer than New York.

Wie bildest du die Steigerungsformen der Adjektive?

- **Einsilbige Adjektive** sowie **zweisilbige** Adjektive auf *-le*, *-er*, *-y* und *-ow* steigerst du, indem du an die Grundform *-er* bzw. *-est* anhängst.
  Beispiel: great → greater → greatest
  Nach einem **kurzen einfachen Vokal** musst du den Endkonsonanten verdoppeln und *-er* oder *-est* anhängen.
  Beispiel: fit → fitter → fittest
  Endet das **Adjektiv auf *-e***, hängst du nur *-r* oder *-st* an.
  Beispiel: nice → nicer → nicest
  Bei **zweisilbigen Adjektiven auf *-y*** wird bei der Steigerung das *-y* zu *-i*.
  Beispiel: lovely → lovelier → loveliest
- **Zweisilbige Adjektive,** die nicht auf *-le*, *-er*, *-y* und *-ow* enden, sowie **mehrsilbige Adjektive** steigerst du, indem du dem Adjektiv *more* bzw. *most* voranstellst.
  Beispiel: fabulous → more fabulous → most fabulous

- Einige Adjektive haben **unregelmäßige Steigerungsformen.** Diese musst du auswendig lernen!

Beispiele:

good	→	better	→	best
bad	→	worse	→	worst
little	→	less	→	least
much/many	→	more	→	most
old	→	older/elder*	→	oldest/eldest*

(* nur für Verwandtschaftsbezeichnungen)

Wie bildest du Vergleiche?

- **Unterschiedliche Dinge** vergleichst du, indem du den Komparativ des Adjektivs mit *than* gebrauchst.

  Beispiel: New York is bigger than London.

- Die **Gleichheit zweier Dinge** wird ausgedrückt mit *as* + Positiv des Adjektivs + *as*

  Beispiel: London is as important as New York.

- Um die **Ungleichheit zweier Dinge** auszudrücken, verwendest du *not* + *as* + Positiv des Adjektivs + *as*

  Beispiel: London is not as big as New York.

Aufgabe 4 Look at the interesting places in New York and London and write about them. Use the comparative and the superlative form of each of the adjectives given.

a) *The World Trade Center was the highest building in New York; it was higher than all the others.*

b) ______

c) ______

d) ______

e) ______

f) ______

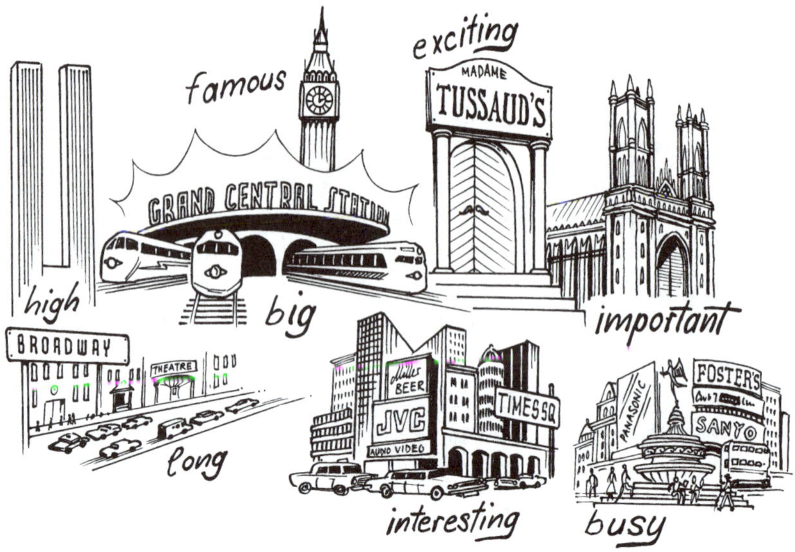

g) ______________________________

h) ______________________________

Aufgabe 5 The following sentences are grammatically correct, but they are a little silly. Find out what is wrong and correct the mistakes.

a) It's absolutely necessary that the poor help the rich.

____

b) The Dutch live in France.

____

c) Everybody likes unfriendly waitresses better than friendly waitresses.

____

d) The young of today will be the old of yesterday.

____

e) The English and the Germans have always lived together peacefully.

____

3.3 *one/ones* beim Adjektiv

Wann verwendest du *one/ones*?

Um die **Wiederholung eines Nomens** zu vermeiden, kannst du **Adjektiven** das **Stützwort** *one* (für Nomen, die im Singular stehen) bzw. *ones* (für Nomen, die im Plural stehen) folgen lassen.

Beispiel: How many towers had the World Trade Center got? It had two identical ones.

Nach einem Komparativ, der mit dem bestimmten Artikel verbunden ist, ist *one/ones* nicht unbedingt nötig, nach einem Superlativ steht das Stützwort meist nicht.

Beispiele: Which of the two towns is the bigger (one): London or New York?
Each of them is the biggest in its country, and there are only few bigger ones in the whole world.

ufgabe 6 Jim always wants to be better than Joe, but he is never lucky. Use the adjectives from the list in the comparative form and write about Jim and Joe. Don't forget *one/ones.*
heavy, clean, nice, intelligent, expensive, happy, big, beautiful, fast, large, interesting, elegant

a)

Jim wears nicer shoes, but Joe wears bigger ones.

b)

____

c)

d)

e)

f)

… rund ums Verb

4 Adverbien

Adverbien sind Wörter wie *very, almost, really*. Sie bestimmen das im Satz genannte Geschehen in Bezug auf die **Zeit**, den **Raum**, die **Qualität** und die **Intensität** näher.

Beispiele:	She saw me at once.	Zeit
	We met there.	Raum
	They talked quickly.	Qualität
	I'm terribly sorry.	Intensität

4.1 Einsatzmöglichkeiten von Adverbien

Wann verwendest du ein Adverb?

Mit einem Adverb *(adverb)* kannst du Näheres über ein **Verb**, ein **Adjektiv** oder ein anderes **Adverb** sagen. Ein Adverb kann sich aber auch auf einen **ganzen Satz** beziehen.

Beispiele:

He swims quickly.
(nähere Bestimmung eines Verbs)

Our tennis coach is really bad.
(nähere Bestimmung eines Adjektivs)

She runs very slowly.
(nähere Bestimmung eines Adverbs)

Unfortunately, she didn't win.
(Aussage über einen Satz)

Wie bildest du Adverbien?

- Die meisten Adverbien werden durch **Anhängen von *-ly*** von Adjektiven abgeleitet.
  Beispiel: beautiful → beautifully
- Andere Adverbien sind so genannte **ursprüngliche Adverbien,** die von keinem anderen Wort abgeleitet sind: *always, often, very, almost, at once, only, after.*
- Von Adjektiven, die auf *-ly* enden, kannst du keine Adverbien bilden, du musst eine **adverbiale Bestimmung** (meist mit dem Zusatz *way*) daraus machen.
  Beispiel: He's always friendly. → He always talks to us in a friendly way.
- Ausnahmen: Adjektive und Adverbien, die die gleiche Form haben.

Beispiele: fast	→	fast	
hard	→	hard	(hardly = ‚kaum')
late	→	late	(lately = ‚kürzlich')
near	→	near	(nearly = ‚fast')

Aufgabe 1 Put in adverbs.

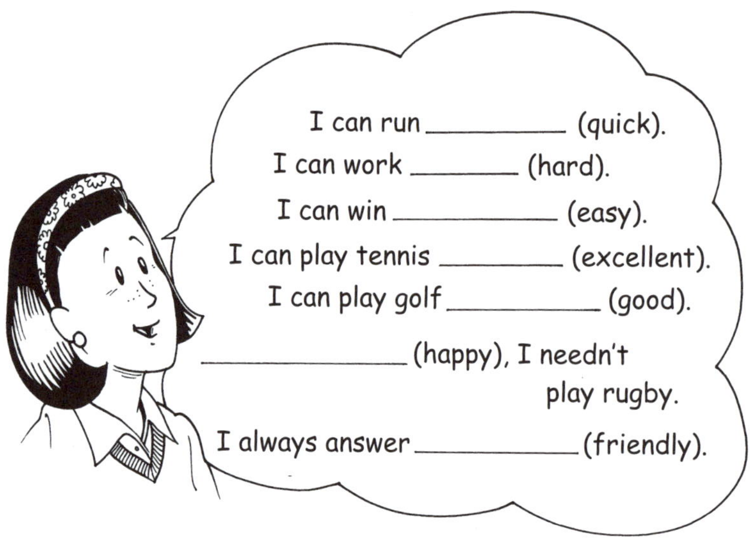

An welche Stelle im Satz stellst du Adverbien?

Ein Wort, das Näheres über eine Handlung aussagt, ist ein **Adverb**. Eine Umstandsbestimmung, die aus mehreren Wörtern besteht, wird **Adverbiale** genannt. Die **Stellung von Adverbien und Adverbialen im Satz** ist abhängig davon, um welche Art von Umstandsbestimmung es sich handelt.

- Adverbialen **des Ortes** und der **bestimmten Zeit** stehen am **Anfang** oder **Ende** des Satzes.

  Beispiele: At school, we have no swimming-pool.
  We got several new coaches last term.

- Stehen am Ende des Satzes mehrere adverbiale Bestimmungen, so steht die **Ortsbestimmung vor** der **Zeitbestimmung.**

  Beispiel: We always go to the public baths on Thursdays.

- Adverbien der **unbestimmten Zeit** (*finally, soon*) und **Häufigkeit** (*sometimes, usually*) stehen bei Zeiten ohne Hilfsverb vor dem Verb, ansonsten nach dem ersten Hilfsverb oder nach einer Form von *to be*.

  Beispiele: The match finally came!
  I've rarely seen such a bad referee.
  The referee was never close to the ball.

  Sometimes, usually, finally und *normally* können auch am Satzanfang stehen.

  Beispiel: Usually, he plays basketball.

- Adverbien der **Art und Weise** stehen meist vor dem Vollverb oder nach dem direkten Objekt.

  Beispiel: I quickly did my homework: I read two pages loudly.

  Hat das Verb allerdings kein Objekt nach sich, steht das Adverb nach dem Verb.

  Beispiel: Then I went to baseball practice by bike.

Aufgabe 2 Find the right positions for the adverbs and adverbials given in brackets.

a) We drove to a soccer match. (in Liverpool, last Saturday)

b) The train was full. (very, unfortunately)

c) It is empty, but everything was different because of the match. (usually, probably, that day)

d) When we arrived, we couldn't get off the train. (finally, at once, in Liverpool, even)

e) So we waited until the other passengers had got off. (at last, angrily)

f) We arrived. (luckily, before 4 o'clock, at the stadium)

g) We went in, and the match started. (immediately, happily)

h) When we went back, we all shouted, because our team had won. (gloriously, two hours later, to the station, cheerfully)

Wie übersetzt du Adverbien?

Ein deutsches Adverb wird im Englischen oft mit einem Verb wiedergegeben, vor allem ‚gern' *to like*, ‚anscheinend' *to seem*, ‚lieber' *to prefer*, ‚wahrscheinlich' *to be likely*, ‚weiterhin' *to continue/go on*, ‚hoffentlich' *I hope* und ‚leider' *I'm afraid*.

Beispiel: Ich gehe gern zum Fußballtraining.
I like going to soccer practice.

Aufgabe 3 Translate.

a) In the past few weeks, we've lost all our matches clearly, I'm afraid.

b) Of course, we would have preferred to play better, but it seems we always play badly.

c) I hope we won't continue to disappoint our fans so much.

d) If we do, we're likely to lose many of our supporters very soon.

4.2 Adverbien – Steigerung und Vergleiche

Wann steigerst du Adverbien und wann verwendest du Vergleiche?

Um vergleichen zu können, **wie** verschiedene Tätigkeiten ausgeführt werden, brauchst du die Steigerungsformen des Adverbs: den Komparativ und den Superlativ. Den Vergleichssatz selbst bildest du wie beim Vergleich mit Adjektiven mit *than, less* oder *(not) as … as* (siehe auch Adjektive S. 27).

Beispiele: Who runs fastest of all? (Steigerung)
I certainly run faster than my brother. (Vergleich)

Wie bildest du Steigerungsformen der Adverbien und wie bildest du Vergleiche?

- Alle abgeleiteten Adverbien werden mit *more/most* gesteigert.
  Beispiel: You ought to play more aggressively.
- Lediglich die wenigen einsilbigen Adverbien werden mit *-er/-est* gesteigert.
  Beispiel: In my class, I work harder than everybody else.
- Beachte die unregelmäßige Steigerung:
  well – better – best
  badly – worse – worst

Aufgabe 4 How well did they do their sports? Compare the two sportsmen in each picture.

a) 

Number six drove ____________
____________________.
(fast)

b) 

____
____________________.
(elegant)

c)

____

______________________________.

(active)

d)

____

______________________________.

(powerful)

e)

____

______________________________.

(hard)

f)

____

______________________________.

(quick)

4.3 Adverb oder Adjektiv?

Wann verwendest du ein Adverb, wann ein Adjektiv?

- Wenn du Näheres über eine Person oder über eine Sache sagen willst (‚**wie ist sie?**'), so verwendest du das **Adjektiv.** Wenn du Näheres über eine Tätigkeit sagen willst (‚**wie wird es getan?**'), so verwendest du das **Adverb.**

  Beispiele: Women are said to be careful drivers.
  But most men drive carefully, too.

- Das **Adverb** kannst du also nur bei Verben, die eine **Tätigkeit oder Handlung** ausdrücken, einsetzen. Wenn ein **Zustand** beschrieben wird, steht das **Adjektiv.**

  Beispiele: Why do they laugh so happily?
  Why are you unhappy?

  Zustandsverben sind z. B.: *to be, to have, to see, to stay, to become, to get*

  Einige Verben können eine Tätigkeit **oder** einen Zustand ausdrücken, z. B. *to look* ‚schauen' – ‚aussehen', *to smell* ‚riechen' (Geruch wahrnehmen) – ‚riechen' (Geruch abgeben), *to taste* ‚schmecken' (Geschmack wahrnehmen) – ‚schmecken' (Geschmack abgeben), *to turn* ‚sich drehen' – ‚werden'. Sie können also, je nach Bedeutung, mit einem Adverb oder einem Adjektiv verbunden werden.

  Beispiel: Don't look so sadly at me! (‚schauen', ‚anschauen')
  He always looks sad. (‚aussehen')

Aufgabe 5 Adjective or adverb? Put in the right forms.

When their team has lost an (important) ____________ [1] match, when a tennis star has played (bad) ____________ [2], when the final results don't sound (fantastic) ____________ [3] at all, coaches always tell their (unhappy) ____________ [4] sportsmen: "If you (real) ____________ [5] want to be (successful) ____________ [6], you have to work (hard) ____________ [7] and you must be prepared for a (long) ____________ [8] wait."
But they can (easy) ____________ [9] talk like that: they needn't perform (good) ____________ [10] while the (noisy) ____________ [11] crowd is cheering (ecstatic) ____________ [12] for their opponent, they needn't run after a ball that (quick) ____________ [13] crosses the line and comes for you at an (incredible) ____________ [14] speed, they needn't listen to (angry) ____________ [15] and (disappointed) ____________ [16] spectators who shout at them (unfriendly) ____________. [17]

What's the use of all the (good) ______________________[18] preparation – where coaches are of course of (invaluable) ______________________[19] help – if you can only act (nervous) ________________[20] as soon as you are on the field? Whether our (dear) ______________[21] coaches believe it or not: all (real) ______________[22] sportsmen – the (absolute) ______________[23] (successful) ________________[24] ones and those who are not so (successful) ______________________[25] – do their very best in every competition!

Tipps zum *story writing*

Für das *story writing* gelten dieselben Grundsätze wie für das Schreiben einer Erlebniserzählung auf Deutsch:

- Eine Geschichte braucht eine **Einleitung**, in der der Leser das Wichtigste über die **Personen**, den **Ort** und die **Zeit** der Handlung erfährt.
- **Wörtliche Rede** macht deine Geschichte lebendiger.
- Versuche möglichst viele **Nomen durch ein Adjektiv und möglichst viele Verben und Adjektive durch ein Adverb zu ergänzen**; auch das macht deine Geschichte anschaulicher.
- **Verbinde deine Sätze** miteinander (Konjunktionen wie *but* oder *after all* helfen dir dabei).
- Verwende viele **Orts- und Zeitangaben**; auch sie können dir dabei helfen, zwei Sätze miteinander zu verbinden (z.B. *in the neighbourhood; later; at the same time*).
- **Lies deine Geschichte mehrmals sorgfältig durch**. Achte dabei in einem Durchgang auf Grammatik und Rechtschreibung. In einem weiteren Durchgang kannst du sicherstellen, dass dir keine inhaltlichen Fehler oder Gedankensprünge passiert sind.

Aufgabe 6* Story writing

Harriet trainiert seit Monaten mit der Hockeymannschaft ihrer Schule für ein großes Turnier in Birmingham. Alles läuft prima, und am Abend vor dem letzten Training schenken ihr ihre Eltern sogar einen neuen Schläger. Doch am nächsten Tag fällt sie unglücklich und kann nicht weiter trainieren. Wird sie am Wochenende spielen können?

Write Harriet's story and find a suitable title and a good ending.

5 Zeiten der Vergangenheit

Willst du von zurückliegenden Handlungen berichten, so benutzt du dazu eine **Zeitform der Vergangenheit**. Die englische Sprache stellt dir dafür die drei Vergangenheitszeiten ***past tense***, ***present perfect*** und ***past perfect*** zur Verfügung. Jede dieser drei Zeitformen ist jeweils in der einfachen **(*simple*)** Form und in der Verlaufsform **(*progressive*)** verwendbar.

Beispiele:	They looked at me.	*(simple past)*
	They were looking at me.	*(past progressive)*
	They have looked at me.	*(present perfect simple)*
	They have been looking at me.	*(present perfect progressive)*
	They had looked at me.	*(past perfect simple)*
	They had been looking at me.	*(past perfect progressive)*

Das System, nach dem du die richtige Zeitform auswählst, ist im Englischen völlig anders als im Deutschen. Deshalb musst du die Regeln besonders gut lernen und einüben.

5.1 *simple past* und *past progressive*

Simple past und *past progressive* sind beides **Zeiten der Vergangenheit** und drücke unterschiedliche Arten von vergangenen Handlungen/Ereignissen aus. Du kannst diese beiden Zeitformen grundsätzlich nur dann verwenden, wenn du **Handlungen** beschreibst, die **in der Vergangenheit begannen** und auch **in der Vergangenheit abgeschlossen** wurden.

Rund ums *simple past*

Wann verwendest du das *simple past?*

- Du verwendest das *simple past* für **einmalige und wiederholte Handlungen** sowie für **Zustände** in der Vergangenheit.
  Als **Signalwörter** können vorkommen: *yesterday, ten years ago, before that, at midnight, after they had …, always, every year* usw.

  Beispiele: I listened to the radio before lunch.
  It rained every day.
  Were you really ill?

- Auch um **Gewohnheiten** auszudrücken, verwendest du das *simple past.*

  Beispiel: When I was on holiday in London, I always paid a visit to my aunt.

- Das *simple past* gebrauchst du auch in Erzählungen für die einzelnen, nach und nach ablaufenden Handlungen.
  Mögliche **Signalwörter:** *at first, then, after that, when, all at once* usw.

  Beispiel: When he came home, he opened the door of his house. Then he switched on the lights, and suddenly he saw it: …

- Auch bei Fragen mit *when* und in den dazugehörigen Antworten benutzt du das *simple past.*

  Beispiel: "When did they go on holiday?" – "I think they left yesterday."

Wie bildest du das *simple past?*

watch	→	watched	Bei regelmäßigen Verben: Infinitiv + *-ed*
carry	→	carried	Nach Konsonanten wird *-y* zu *-ie.*
stop	→	stopped	Nach kurzem betonten Vokal wird der Endkonsonant verdoppelt.
like	→	liked	Nach stimmlosem Konsonant wird *-d* als [t] gesprochen.
want	→	wanted	Nach *-t, -d* wird *-ed* als [ɪd] gesprochen.

- Bei den **unregelmäßigen Verben** gibt es keine einheitliche Bildungsweise. Du musst die unregelmäßigen Verben systematisch lernen und immer wieder üben. Eine Liste findest du in deinem Lehrbuch.
  go → went
- Die **modalen Hilfsverben** werden im *past tense* folgendermaßen umschrieben:
  can → was/were able to
  may → was/were allowed to
  must → had to

ufgabe 1 Complete the crossword puzzle with the *simple past* forms of the following verbs:

across:

3 cut
4 eat
6 have
9 be
10 begin
12 sit
13 do
17 think
18 forget
19 wake
20 read

down:

1 come
2 tear
5 hear
7 go
8 buy
11 stand
14 take
15 give
16 tell

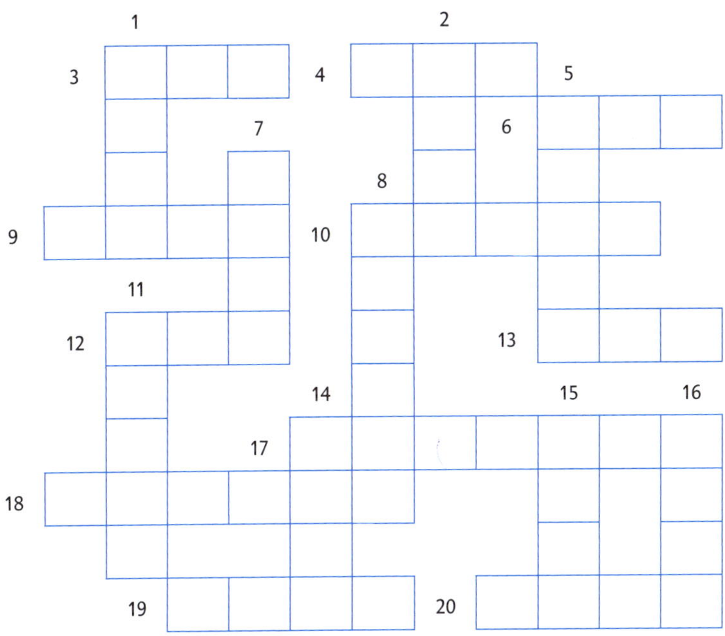

Aufgabe 2 Put the following story into *simple past!* In the first few sentences I have underlined the verbs which you must change.

In their holidays, Rachel and Peter <u>are</u> in a hotel near a lake where they <u>may</u> go swimming every day. Of course, their mother <u>must</u> be with them. They <u>try</u> to get up early every day. Rachel always wants to go surfing, but one day Peter has another idea. He cycles to a nearby village because there is a farm with beautiful horses there. From that day on, he goes to the farm every morning, and he stays there for two hours. Then he rushes back to the hotel, and later, he has breakfast with his sister and his mother. Sometimes, of course, they all do something together; they climb a mountain or fly a kite. But on other days, they only go to the beach, lie down there and read a book or talk to each other or do nothing all day. The children really enjoy their holidays!

ufgabe 3 Judy, a girl from Liverpool, writes a letter to one of her friends and tells her about her last summer holidays. Of course, she spent them in Great Britain (you can choose where). Write Judy's letter. Use as many *simple past* forms as you can. Don't forget that her friend really wants to know everything about Judy's holidays: where she went, where she stayed, who was with her, what she did, …

You will find hints on writing a personal letter on page 194/195.

Bei **Verneinungen, Fragen** und **Kurzantworten** musst du im *simple past* das **Hilfsverb** *to do* verwenden.

Beispiel: I didn't ask him, he asked me!
"Did you meet him the day before yesterday?"
"Yes, I did."

Ausnahmen sind

- das Verb *to be*

  Beispiel: I wasn't invited last year.

- das Verb *have got*

  Beispiel: You hadn't got an invitation.

- Fragen mit den Fragewörtern *who* und *what*, wenn sie nach dem Subjekt fragen (‚wer?', ‚was?').

  Beispiel: Who arrived at three o'clock?

Aufgabe 4 What can you do in New York? Here's a list of activities for a visit to New York. Mary was in New York last June. She had this list with her and ticked off everything she did. Now her friends want to know if she did it all. Ask their questions and give Mary's answers.

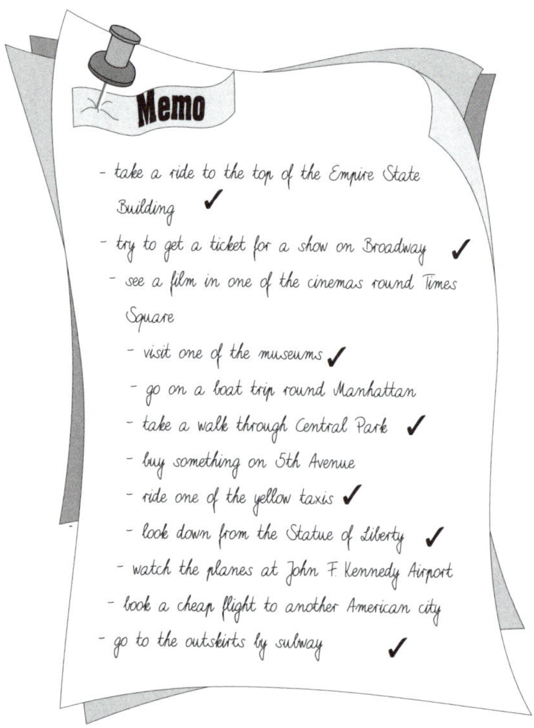

a) "Did you take a ride to the top of the Empire State Building?"
"Yes, I did. I took a ride to the top of the Empire State Building."

b)

c)

d)

e)

f)

g)

h)

i)

j)

k)

l)

Aufgabe 5

a) Put in the *simple past* forms of the verbs.

Peter ___saw___ [1] (see) David *on the beach.*

He ____________ [2] (say) *something* to him.

But David ____________ [3] (not answer), *because he never listens to Peter*

They ____________ [4] (not be) really *friends* after all.

But *Peter* ____________ [5] (be) very angry, and he ____________ [6] (go) red in the face.

Suddenly, he ____________ [7] (can) see *another friend of his.*

Then he ____________ [8] (start) running to *the sea.*

A few moments later, Anne ____________ [9] (come).

No, they ____________ [10] (not go) home together.

Anne ____________ [11] (can) stay *until eight*, but *Peter* ____________ [12] (cannot) stay so long.

b) Ask for the parts of the sentences on the left which are printed in italics.

Where did Peter see David?

____

____

____

____

____

____

____

____

____

____

____

____

____

____

____

____

____

____

____

____

____

____

____

____

Rund ums *past progressive*

Wann verwendest du das *past progressive?*

- Das *past progressive* brauchst du immer dann, wenn **mehrere Handlungen** in **der Vergangenheit teilweise gleichzeitig ablaufen**. Die länger andauernde Handlung steht dann im *past progressive.*
  Mögliche **Signalwörter:** *while, when* usw.
  Beispiel: She entered the room and saw that the children were playing.
- In Erzählungen verwendest du das *past progressive* für **Hintergrundhandlungen** und **Beschreibungen**, also auch für die Einleitung vor dem eigentlichen Beginn der Geschichte. Im Unterschied dazu steht die eigentliche Handlung der Geschichte, die Geschehnisse also, die nach und nach ablaufen, im *simple past.*
  Mögliche **Signalwörter**: *when, while* usw.
  Beispiel: The sun was shining. A lot of people were lying on the beach. Suddenly, a tall man ran towards me. He wasn't wearing much, and I saw that he was trembling. When he reached me, he shouted something at me, but I couldn't understand him. Everybody was looking at him, and at last I said: "Go away, I don't know you!"
- Bei Verben, die einen Zustand ausdrücken, darfst du das *past progressive* nicht verwenden, also z. B. bei *to be, to have* (aber *progressive* möglich in der Bedeutung ‚essen', ‚trinken'), *to want, to like, to love, to hate, to think* (aber *progressive* möglich in der Bedeutung ‚nachdenken'), *to be allowed to, to be able to, to have to, to understand.* Dies gilt auch in den anderen Vergangenheitszeiten, vgl. S. 51 und 59).
  Beispiel: While I was in Hollywood, I met Whoopi Goldberg.

Wie bildest du das *past progressive?*

- ***past*-Form von *to be* + *ing*-Form des Verbs.**
  Beispiele: I/he/she/it was running.
  you/we/you/they were shouting.
- **Nach kurzem, betonten Vokal** wird der **Endkonsonant verdoppelt**.
  Beispiel: sit → sitting
- Stummes ***-e* am Ende entfällt.**
  Beispiel: give → giving
- ***-ie* am Ende** wird zu ***-y***.
  Beispiel: lie → lying
- *Die* **Verneinung** bildest du mit ***wasn't*** bzw. ***weren't***.
  Beispiel: They weren't sleeping.

Aufgabe 6 Write down what the Riley family were doing when the telephone rang.

a) Martin was cleaning / tidying his room.

b) ______

c) ______

d) ______

e) ______

f) ______

g) ______

Aufgabe 7 **Mixed exercise:** Put the verbs in brackets into the correct tenses: *simple past* or *past progressive.*

Mr Black ______ [1] (not, to be) a rich man. So he ______ [2] (like) betting at horse-races. One Sunday, he ______ [3] (decide) at the very last moment, when the horses ______ [4] (already, get) ready to start, to bet on a horse which nobody ______ [5] (think) to be a favourite. Who ______ [6] (win) the race? Believe it or not – this horse ______ [7] (do), and Mr Black ______ [8] (get) a lot of money.

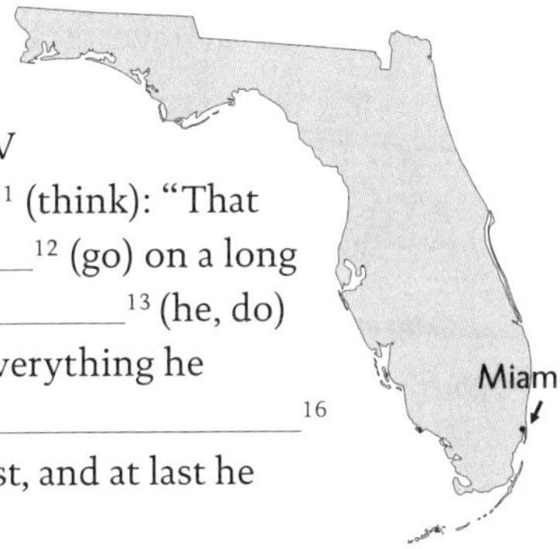

While he ____________ [9] (think) about what to do with that money, he suddenly ____________ [10] (remember) a TV advert for Florida, and he ____________ [11] (think): "That is where I will go!" So he ____________ [12] (go) on a long holiday to the USA. And what ____________ [13] (he, do) there? Well, he ____________ [14] (see) everything he ____________ [15] (want) to see: he ____________ [16] (travel) from north to south, from east to west, and at last he ____________ [17] (arrive) in Miami.
But when he ____________ [18] (step) out of his car, it ____________ [19] (start) to rain, and it ____________ [20] (turn) cold. Mr Black ____________ [21] (only, wear) a T-shirt and short trousers, so he ____________ [22] (soon, have) goose-pimples all over his arms and legs.
But he ____________ [23] (not mind). Do you know where he ____________ [24] (go)? He ____________ [25] (drive) straight to the most expensive shop in the city and ____________ [26] (buy) everything he ____________ [27] (need) – he ____________ [28] (not have to) be careful with his money! A few hours later, he ____________ [29] (take) a first-class flight back to England, and in the end, he ____________ [30] (be) happy to be back home.
The next day, he ____________ [31] (tell) me all about his trip. I ____________ [32] (ring) him up at 11 o'clock in the morning, and what ____________ [33] (he, do)? He ____________ [34] (still, lie) in bed and ____________ [35] (sleep)! He still ____________ [36] (think) that he ____________ [37] (be) on holiday!

Aufgabe 8 Ask questions with *simple past* and *past progressive* in one sentence.

a) you – drop the picture / you – tidy your room
Did you drop the picture when you were tidying your room?

b) they – do at five o'clock yesterday / aunt – arrive

c) your parents – sleep / you – come back from the party

d) who – read the news / she – turn on the TV

e) you – meet her / you – go to the cinema

f) your mother – work in the garden / I – ring you up

g) John – visit the castles on his way / he – drive to his aunt's

h) they – hear the loud noise / they – play in the garden

Aufgabe 9 Translate.

Unser diesjähriger Urlaub war schrecklich. In den Jahren zuvor mussten wir gewöhnlich mit unseren Eltern fahren, doch dieses Jahr durften wir alleine mit dem Zug fahren. Als wir im Zug saßen, kam der Schaffner und wollte unsere Fahrkarten sehen. Als mein Bruder Jeff sie nicht sofort finden konnte, wollte uns der Schaffner beim nächsten Bahnhof aus dem Zug werfen. Doch glücklicherweise fand ich die Fahrkarten in meiner Hosentasche. Auch in der Pension hatten wir Schwierigkeiten: Die Wirtin wollte uns ein kleines Zimmer geben. Wir redeten gerade noch mit ihr, als ein anderer Mann hinter uns sagte: „Kinder sollten in der Jugendherberge schlafen!“ Aber schließlich konnten wir sie überzeugen und sie gab uns die Zimmerschlüssel. Fünf Minuten später waren wir schon beim Kofferauspacken. Das war noch nicht alles: Es geschah so viel Schlimmes in diesem Urlaub, dass wir die Pension früher als geplant verließen und so schnell wie möglich wieder nach Hause fuhren.

5.2 *present perfect simple* und *present perfect progressive*

Das ***present perfect*** wird für Vorgänge und Zustände verwendet, die vergangen sind, aber einen **Bezug zur Gegenwart** haben.

Rund ums *present perfect simple*

Wann verwendest du das *present perfect simple*?

- Du verwendest das *present perfect simple* für Handlungen, die in der Vergangenheit abgeschlossen wurden, die aber eine **Auswirkung auf die Gegenwart** haben. Das Ergebnis der Handlung ist also in der Gegenwart des Sprechenden sichtbar (*resultative present perfect*) und das ist auch der Grund, warum er davon spricht.

  Beispiel: She has cancelled the flight. (= She can't fly now.)

- Du gebrauchst das *present perfect simple* auch **für Handlungen, die gerade erst abgeschlossen wurden**. Mögliche **Signalwörter**: *just* usw.

  Beispiel: She has just taken the suitcase out of the boot.
  (= It isn't inside any more.)

- Auch für **Dinge, die noch nicht passiert sind**, musst du das *present perfect simple* verwenden. Mögliche **Signalwörter**: *never, not … yet, not … so far* usw.

  Beispiel: I've never been to New York.
  (= I don't know anything about it.)

- Du benutzt das *present perfect simple* auch, um zu fragen, ob etwas bis zum Sprechzeitpunkt schon einmal passiert ist.
  Mögliche **Signalwörter**: *already, ever, yet* usw.

  Beispiel: Has he ever packed a suitcase himself?
  (= Does he know how to pack a suitcase?)

- Das *present perfect simple* kann an die Stelle des *present perfect progressive* treten, und zwar bei **Zustandsverben**, also Verben der **Sinneswahrnehmung** (*to see, to hear, to notice, to feel, to smell, to look* usw.), Verben der **Meinungs- und Wunschäußerung** (*to know, to think, to want, to wish* usw.) und anderen Verben, bei denen kein Verlauf einer Handlung ausgedrückt werden kann (z. B. *to be, to have, to belong, to seem, to mean, to sound, to live, to love, to hate, to dislike*).

  Beispiel: I've heard them since midnight.

Wie bildest du das *present perfect simple?*

have/has + past participle; Verneinung: *haven't/hasn't + past participle*

Beispiel: I/you/we/you/they have he/she/it has watched.

Regelmäßig wird das *past participle* auf ***-ed*** gebildet, wobei dieselben Regeln gelten wie für die Bildung des *simple past* auf *-ed* (vgl. S. 40).

Die **unregelmäßigen Verben** (sowohl *past*-Form als auch *past participle*) musst du **auswendig lernen**. Eine Liste findest du in deinem Lehrbuch.

Aufgabe 10 Write down what Randy has done and what she hasn't done.

- arrive at her hotel
- unpack her suitcase
- put her shoes in the wardrobe
- buy a postcard
- eat all her biscuits
- start to read a book

a) *She has arrived at her hotel.*

b) ______

c) ______

d) ______

e) ______

f) ______

fgabe 11 Say it again in other words. Use the verbs from the list to make sentences in the *present perfect simple*: *~~go~~, put, forget, lose, come, go, taste, go, send, see, check.*

a) They are on holiday in Italy.
They've gone to Italy on holiday.

b) Sorry, my book is at home.

c) You had my watch. Where is it now?

d) Is anybody here?

e) I don't know if this lemonade is good.

f) Where are you?

g) Next week, I'll see "Cats" at last.

h) The passengers aren't here now.

i) I'm afraid I can't find my money.

j) Your tyres are okay.

k) We have no reservation from you.

Rund ums *present perfect progressive*

Wann verwendest du das *present perfect progressive?*

- Das *present perfect progressive* betont – im Gegensatz zum *present perfect simple* –, dass die Handlung bzw. der Vorgang noch nicht abgeschlossen ist oder gerade erst beendet wurde.
  Mögliche **Signalwörter:** *all day, this whole week, up to now* usw.
  Beispiele: What have you been doing all day?
  I haven't been reading! I've been watching TV.
- Folgende Verben, die einen längeren Vorgang beschreiben, werden sehr häufig im *present perfect progressive* benutzt: *sit, live, stay, stand, hang, wait, spend, work, try* usw.
  Beispiel: She has been sitting on the beach all afternoon.
- Das deutsche ‚**seit**' wird im Englischen mit ***for*** übersetzt, wenn es eine **Zeitspanne** beschreibt, mit ***since***, wenn von dem **Zeitpunkt** die Rede ist, zu dem die Handlung begann.
  Beispiele: They have been playing for three hours.
  They have been playing since two o'clock.

Wie bildest du das *present perfect progressive?*

have/has + been + present participle (*ing*-Form des Verbs);
Verneinung: *haven't/hasn't + been + present participle*

Beispiel: I/you/we/you/they have he/she/it has been running

Aufgabe 12 Write down what they have been doing until now.

a) 

Mr Snider ______________________
pictures all day.

b) 

Toby ______________________
for an hour.

c) 

The mole ______________________ holes since 11 o'clock.

d) 

The Porters ______________________ all Saturday.

e) 

The children ______________________ all afternoon.

f) 

The water ______________________ since 8 o'clock.

ufgabe 13 Complete the following sentences with suitable verbs in the *present perfect progressive* and put in *since* or *for*. Choose from the list, and be careful: there are more verbs than you need, but you may use each verb only once!
dance, swim, play, clean, read, sit, try, wash, tidy, talk, rain, understand, think, do, look for, watch.

a) She ______________ her newspaper ______________ two hours now.

b) They ______________ in the garden ______________ three o'clock.

c) I ______________ the car all morning.

d) ________________ (you) the dishes ________________ one hour?

e) We ________________ (not) games all evening, we ________________.

f) He ________________ in the lake ________________ quarter past nine.

g) What ________________ (they) in that church?

h) ________________ (you, not) your room ________________ you woke up?

i) It ________________ cats and dogs ________________ nearly two days now.

Aufgabe 14 *Present perfect simple* or *progressive?* Make 10 sentences.

I	drive	the house		two o'clock.
You	live	our car		all day.
He	be	in London		five years ago.
She	look at	all the sights		twenty minutes.
Mrs Baker	belong	at	since	you last saw me.
This garden	work	in	for	yesterday.
We	never have to	records		an hour and a half.
They	listen	Tower Bridge		these past few years.
My parents	go	to …		for years.
The Greens	see	alone for so long		all my life.

Mrs Baker has been looking at all the sights for an hour and a half.

____

____

____

____

____

____

____

____

____

fgabe 15

Before the Wilsons drive to Yosemite National Park on Sunday, Mr Wilson wants to know from his wife and his children if everything in the house is okay. Here is what they say. Find suitable verbs and complete the dialogue in the *present perfect* (positive or negative). Try to use every verb only once.

Mr Wilson: Aren't the windows open?
Mrs Wilson: No, I have closed them.
Mr Wilson: Is the floor clean?
Robert: Yes, I ______________[1] it for half an hour.
Mr Wilson: Have the fish enough food?
Jenny: Yes, I ______________[2] them.
Mr Wilson: Are your clothes in the wardrobe?
Robert: Yes, I ___________________[3] my clothes in my wardrobe, but I ________________[4] your clothes on the bed.
Mr Wilson: Aren't the cups and plates still standing on the table in the dining-room?
Mrs Wilson: No, Robert ______________[5] them into the kitchen.
Mr Wilson: And you've left them in the kitchen, dirty, haven't you?
Robert: No, we ________________[6] them up, but we _______________[7] them away.
Mr Wilson: Have we got a few sandwiches?
Mrs Wilson: No, I ___________________[8] any because I _________________[9] since eight o'clock.
Mr Wilson: And where is my gold watch? ________________[10] (you, see) it?
Mrs Wilson: Yes, Robert _________________[11] it.
Mr Wilson: Have you got the keys? I _____________________[12] for them for twenty minutes.
Jenny: Yes, I ______________[13] them on the bookshelf.
Mr Wilson: And why aren't the suitcases in the boot?
Robert: Because I ______________[14] time to put them in.
Mr Wilson: Why not? What ______________[15] (you, do) all the time?
Robert: Oh, Dad, don't make me angry. I certainly _________________[16] (sleep)!
Mr Wilson: Okay, let's go then.

Aufgabe 16 Translate.

Letztes Jahr fuhr Frau Kent, die Frau unseres Metzgers, alleine in den Urlaub, weil ihr Mann das Geschäft nicht schließen wollte. Sie sagte: „Ich habe ein so günstiges Angebot für einen Flug nach Kalifornien in der Zeitung gefunden! Wir waren noch nie in Kalifornien und alle unsere Kunden sagen, dass das die billigste Amerikareise seit Jahren ist!" Also ließ Herr Kent sie fahren, obwohl er nicht gerne allein zu Hause blieb. Bevor sie losfuhr, musste sie zur Bank gehen und Geld umtauschen. Gerade als der Bankangestellte ihr ihre Dollar-Scheine geben wollte, fing ein anderer Kunde zu reden an. Er sagte: „Ich fand es immer großartig, wenn ich in Amerika war. Ich weiß, wovon ich rede: ich habe schon achtmal meinen Urlaub dort verbracht und ich komme gerade wieder aus New York zurück." „Wirklich?" fragte Frau Kent ihn. „Dann müssen Sie mir alles über das Land und die Leute erzählen! Waren die Menschen immer freundlich zu Ihnen? Hatten Sie jemals Probleme mit der Polizei? Welche Sehenswürdigkeiten haben Sie schon angeschaut? Hatten Sie einen guten Flug? Wer hat Ihnen geholfen, wenn Sie in Schwierigkeiten waren? Welche Städte gefielen Ihnen am besten? …"

5.3 *past perfect simple* und *past perfect progressive*

Während *past tense* und *present perfect* eine vergangene Handlung in Beziehung zur Gegenwart des Sprechers setzen (vorher abgeschlossen, bis zu dieser Gegenwart heranreichend oder in diese Gegenwart hineinwirkend), stellt das ***past perfect*** einen **Bezug zwischen zwei vergangenen Handlungen** her und sagt aus, dass **eine Handlung vor einer anderen, ebenfalls schon vergangenen Handlung stattfand**. Dementsprechend kommt das *past perfect* meist in einem Satzgefüge vor; die andere – spätere – Handlung steht in der Regel im *simple past*.

Beispiel: At last, the taxi arrived. We had been waiting for it for nearly an hour.

Mit dieser Regel lässt sich auch die Verwendung des *past perfect* in der indirekten Rede bei einem einleitenden Satz in der Vergangenheit erklären: Was für den Sprecher, der in der Vergangenheit redete, schon vergangen war, ist aus gegenwärtiger Sicht **Vorvergangenheit** (vgl. Kapitel 13, S. 155).

Beispiel: They said: "We met Mr Miller on the beach."
They said they had met Mr Miller on the beach.

Rund ums *past perfect simple*

Wann verwendest du das *past perfect simple?*

- Entsprechend dem *simple past* steht das *past perfect simple* **für einmalige oder wiederholte Handlungen in der Vergangenheit, die vor einer anderen abgeschlossen waren**. Achtung: Die spätere Handlung (die im *simple past* steht) steht nicht unbedingt immer im selben Satz.
Mögliche **Schlüsselwörter**: *before, after, when* usw.

  Beispiel: They had spent their holidays at Yellowstone every year for nearly a decade, but now they wanted a change.

- Entsprechend dem *simple past* und dem *present perfect simple* wird das *past perfect simple* anstelle des *past perfect progressive* bei Zustandsverben gebraucht (vgl. auch S. 47 und S. 51).

  Beispiel: We hadn't been on the beach for long when it started to rain.

Wie bildest du das *past perfect simple?*

had + *past participle*; Verneinung: *hadn't* + *past participle*

Beispiel: I/you/he/she/it/we/you/they had played

Regelmäßig wird das *past participle* auf ***-ed*** gebildet, wobei dieselben Regeln gelten wie für die Bildung des *past tense* auf *-ed* (vgl. S. 40).

Die **unregelmäßigen Verben** (sowohl *past*-Form als auch *past participle*) musst du **auswendig lernen**. Eine Liste findest du in deinem Lehrbuch.

Aufgabe 17 Do you remember what Mary did in New York? Look again at exercise 4, page 44, and write down what she did (in the order of her list).

a) After Mary *had taken* a ride to the top of the Empire State Building, she *tried to get* a ticket for a show on Broadway.

b) After she ______________ to get a ticket, she ______________ one of the museums.

c) When ______________ museums, ______________ Central Park.

d) ____

e) ____

f) ____

Aufgabe 18 Answer the following questions in the *past perfect*. Here are some ideas to help you: *not think of that possibility; not ask parents early enough; cousin tells about New York; hear many terrible stories; not be in the USA before; not try to get a ticket early enough; write they will be on holiday at that time; read a lot of beautiful books; everybody asks for presents; not think New York is so great; not like the flight.*

a) Why didn't you go to Chicago?
Because I had heard so many terrible stories about the city.

b) Why did you want to spend your holidays in the USA?
____

c) Why did your friends not come with you?
____

d) Why did you go to New York first?
____

e) Why didn't you go and see a show on Broadway?
____

f) Why didn't you leave for Denver as early as you had planned?
____

g) Why did you go back by ship?

____

h) Why did you take so many photos?

____

i) Why didn't you visit your friends in Houston?

____

j) Why didn't you rent a car?

____

k) Why did you bring so many presents?

____

Rund ums *past perfect progressive*

Wann verwendest du das *past perfect progressive?*

- Das *past perfect progressive* betont – wie alle *progressive*-Formen – die **Dauer eines Vorgangs**. Dieser reicht bis zu einer anderen vergangenen Handlung heran.

  Beispiel: At last we could take the lift to the top of the Empire State Building; we had been queuing for nearly half an hour.

- In der indirekten Rede mit einem einleitenden Verb im *simple past, past perfect* oder *conditional* ist das *past perfect progressive* die einzig mögliche Verlaufsform der Vergangenheit (vgl. S. 155).

  Beispiel: She asked me: "What were you visiting at 4 o'clock?"
  She asked me what I had been visiting at 4 o'clock.

Wie bildest du das *past perfect progressive?*

had been + present participle; Verneinung: *hadn't been + present participle*

Beispiel: I/you/he/she/it/we/you/they had been ringing the bell.

Zu Unregelmäßigkeiten bei der Bildung der *ing*-Form vgl. S. 47.

Aufgabe 19 What had the people at the pier been doing before their boat took off at 2 p.m.? Use *past perfect progressive* with the verbs in brackets, and put in *since* or *for*, too.

a) Three children ____________ (to play) ____________ twenty minutes.

b) Two men ________________ (to talk) ____________ 1.30.

c) A cat ________________ (to wash) itself ______________ fifteen minutes.

d) A cleaner ____________ (to clean) the pier ____________ half an hour.

e) Seagulls ____________ (to fly) above the pier ____________ 12 o'clock.

f) Two women ______________________ (to stand) in front of the house ________________ twenty-five minutes.

Aufgabe 20 Have a look again at exercise 6, page 48.
Nobody in the house answered the phone, so Mr Miller (who had phoned) drove to the Rileys' to ask them why. Write down what they had been doing before the telephone rang.

a) Martin *had been cleaning his room before the telephone rang.*

b) Mrs Riley ____

c) Mr Riley ____

d) Dick and Paul ____________________________________

e) Sooty ____

f) Sally ____

g) Mickey and Mince _________________________________

Aufgabe 21* *Past perfect simple* or *progressive?* Make one sentence out of each pair.

a) We looked down from the Empire State Building for an hour. Then we met Aunt Evelyn.

b) She lived in Detroit since the beginning of her studies at university. Ten years later, she moved to Cincinnati.

c) They walked through Central Park from six to eight. At eight, they took a taxi to their hotel.

d) I knew that theatre for years. Yesterday I saw it for the first time since its renovation.

e) My brother read a book between breakfast and lunchtime. For lunch, we had pizza.

f) Last week, you came back home. Were you on holiday until last week?

g) I waited for my friend for an hour, until half past eight. The performance began at half past eight.

h) He bought a new suit last week. After that, he drove to California.

i) Patty prepared sandwiches for two hours. Then she started making tea.

j) She didn't look nice until yesterday. That's when she went to the hairdresser's.

k) Mike cooked from eleven to twelve. At twelve, he rang up his mother.

a) *We had been looking down from the Empire State Building for an hour when we met Aunt Evelyn.*

b) ____________________

c) ____________________

d) ____________________

e) ____________________

f) ____________________

g) ____________________

h) ____________________

i) ____________________

j) ____________________

k) ____________________

Aufgabe 22* **Mixed exercise:** *Past perfect* or *present perfect*? Put in *have, has* or *had.*

A visit to the Guggenheim Museum, New York.

Charly, who __________[1] already been to the Guggenheim Museum several times, is guiding a few of his friends through the exhibition. "When I came here for the first time, I __________[2] never been to a museum before. Meanwhile I __________[3] come to like museums because I like this one so much. All the pictures you __________[4] been looking at so far are part of the collection of Solomon R. Guggenheim. He __________[5] been collecting works of art for several years before he had the idea of building a museum. He __________[6] made the acquaintance of Frank Lloyd Wright, the architect, who also made plans for an annex, which __________[7] meanwhile been built. Since it was built, the Guggenheim Museum __________[8] been seen worldwide as one of the most interesting museums, and millions of visitors __________[9] come who __________[10] heard about it in their countries. Once when I came here, I __________[11] been touring Manhattan for several hours, and was really tired, but in here I really relaxed. This is why I __________[12] come back here so often."

Aufgabe 23* Put the verbs in brackets into the correct past tenses and fill in *since* or *for.*

JOHN: Where __________[1] (you, spend) your last summer holidays, Ann?

ANN: Well, after I __________[2] (spend) three weeks in Scotland, I __________[3] (stay) in London __________[4] a week. I __________[6] (not be) there __________[7] ten years.

JOHN: But __________[8] (you, not tell) me before you __________[9] (leave) that you'd stay in London only two or three days?

ANN: That's right. I __________[10] (originally, book) two days in London, but then, after I __________[11] (come) back from a sightseeing tour, the people in the hotel __________[12] (tell) me that I __________[13] (can) stay longer. And it __________[14] (be) great there. I __________[15] (never, see) a town more beautiful than London.

JOHN: Well, I think I must go there some day, too. You __________[16] (speak) about London so often now, and just now you __________[17] (become) so excited while you __________[18] (talk) about the town, it must really be wonderful. Do you know that you __________[19] (describe) it to me __________[20] nearly ten minutes?

ANN: Oh, really? Well, it really is fantastic. You know, I ____________[21] (talk) to my colleagues about London, too, all the time ____________[22] I ____________[23] (come) back.

JOHN: By the way, when ____________[24] (you, come) back?

ANN: Last Monday. I ____________[25] (work) again ____________[26] a whole week now.

JOHN: And what ____________[27] (be) the flight like? ____________[28] (you, not be) afraid of it because you ____________[29] (never, fly) before?

ANN: Well, I ____________[30] (have) no problems at all. Okay, it's true, I ____________[31] (tremble) a bit ____________[32] several hours before the plane ____________[33] (take) off, but then I ____________[34] (really, like) the flight. While we ____________[35] (fly), the stewardesses ____________[36] (serve) us a few drinks, and we ____________[37] (also get) a good hot meal. Only the takeoff ____________[38] (not be) a real pleasure: when the plane ____________[39] (take) off, one of the engines suddenly ____________[40] (start) to howl really loud, and of course everybody ____________[41] (want) to know what ____________[42] (go) on, but the pilot ____________[43] (calm) us down at once. But, I ____________[44] (not, hear) anything about you so far. What ____________[45] (you, do) all the time ____________[46] I last ____________[47] (see) you?

JOHN: Not very much. I ____________[48] (buy) myself a new car last week, they ____________[49] (deliver) it to me yesterday. I ____________[50] (really, look) for a nice car ____________[51] nearly six months, but now I still ____________[52] (not, have) the time to try it out. I ____________[53] (absolutely, have to) buy a new one. Do you want to come with me on a short trip out into the country?

ANN: Sorry, I can't. I ____________[54] (repair) and ____________[55] (clean) my bike all afternoon, I'm really too tired now to do much more. And I want to take a bath because I ____________[56] (not, take) one ____________[57] four weeks!

Aufgabe 24 A conversation between a young lady and a young man on a Circle Line Boat on a trip round Manhattan. Here are the young lady's answers – ask the young man's questions (clues for his questions are underlined).

a) "Have you been to the top of the Statue of Liberty yet?"
"No, I haven't been to the top of the Statue of Liberty yet."

b) ______
"No, I saw 'The Lion King' two years ago."

c) ______
"A friend of mine had booked the tickets for me."

d) ______
"I was looking at the skyline when you started talking to me."

e) ______
"I had been listening to a Rod Stewart CD before the trip started."

f) ______
"This woman has been reading since the beginning of the trip."

g) ______
"No, I haven't had lunch yet."

h) ______
"I haven't had lunch yet because I had been working until one o'clock, when the trip started."

i) ______
"No, I didn't go to the movies last week, because I had to go abroad."

j) ______
"I had to go to London."

fgabe 25 Translate.

Waren Sie schon jemals in New York? Ich habe die Stadt letztes Jahr mit ein paar Freunden von mir besucht und sie hat mir sehr gut gefallen. Ich hatte nie zuvor eine solch große Stadt gesehen. Nachdem wir unsere Koffer ausgepackt hatten, machten wir einen Spaziergang im Central Park, weil wir zu müde waren, um eine große Stadtrundfahrt zu unternehmen. In den nächsten Tagen besichtigten wir dann alles, wovon unsere Bekannten und Verwandten seit Jahren erzählten. Aber die miserable Luft störte uns immer wieder. In Irland, wo wir ein Jahr zuvor unseren Urlaub in einem kleinen Dorf verbracht hatten, ist die Luft viel besser. Und es gibt dort viele Tiere, nicht nur Autos. Trotzdem konnten wir verstehen, dass die New Yorker gerne in ihrer Stadt leben, denn wir hatten viele schöne Erlebnisse, die wir sicherlich nicht vergessen werden.

fgabe 26* British English (BE) – American English (AE)

Mr Barton from England was visiting his American friends in Austin, Texas. One night, he had a strange dream. When he wanted to tell his friends this dream, they didn't understand him at once, because he used a lot of British words. Help him and rewrite his dream, replacing the BE words in brackets with AE words (you will find some of them in the picture) and using the right tenses for the verbs given in brackets. Perhaps you can also find the two words which are written differently in AE.

- sidewalk
- skyscraper
- crossing
- subway
- sixth floor
- movies
- truck
- gas station
- trailer
- apartment

It ___________[1] (be) late in the afternoon, on a nice day in ___________[2] (autumn). I ___________[3] (stand) on the ___________[4] (pavement) in front of a ___________[5] (high-rise building) at a ___________[6] (crossroads) in the centre of New York. I ___________[7] (be) about to go to the ___________[8] (Underground) when I ___________[9] (hear) a voice coming from the ___________[10] (fifth floor) of the building. It ___________[11] (be) my daughter – but I ___________[12] (think) she ___________[13] (be) at the ___________[14] (cinema) at that moment! As I ___________[15] (not, understand) what she ___________[16] (say) because a ___________[17] (lorry) ___________[18] (drive) past, I ___________[19] (make) a sign to her, but she ___________[20] (already, disappear). So I ___________[21] (go) to get my car, which I ___________[22] (park) in a ___________[23] (car park) the night before, and drove to a ___________[24] (filling station). There I ___________[25] (meet) a few ___________[26] (pupils) and their ___________[27] (headmaster); they ___________[28] (work) on a ___________[29] (caravan) there. I ___________[30] (never, see) colours like that before! I ___________[31] (ask) them: "How long ___________[32] (you, work) here?", and they ___________[33] (answer): "Never mind! Go back to your ___________[34] (flat) and wake up!" – and that's what I ___________[35] (do).

6 Zeiten der Zukunft

Während es im Deutschen meist möglich ist, das Verb im Präsens zu belassen, wenn von zukünftigem Geschehen die Rede ist, werden im Englischen in solchen Sätzen weitaus häufiger echte **Futurformen** verwendet.

Beispiel: I'm sure (that) it will rain tomorrow.
Ich bin sicher, dass es morgen regnet.

6.1 *will-future*

Wann verwendest du das *will-future?*

Vorhersagen, **Vermutungen, spontane Willenserklärungen** und **künftige Geschehen, die der Sprecher nicht beeinflussen kann**, drückst du mit dem *will-future* aus. Mögliche **Signalwörter:** *I hope, I'm sure, certainly* usw.

Beispiele: They won't come back soon.
She'll probably help us.
Okay, I'll come with you.
The earth will always turn round the sun.

Wie bildest du das *will-future?*

will + Infinitiv des Verbs; Verneinung: *will not* + Infinitiv

Beispiel: I/you/he/she/it/we/you/they will go.

In der **Umgangssprache** wird *I will* oft zu *I'll* und *I will not* zu *I won't*.

Bei den **modalen Hilfsverben** musst du zur Bildung des *will-future* die Ersatzformen verwenden.

Beispiel: They will have to believe me.

Aufgabe 1 You are at a fortune teller's, and she tells you everything about your future. Write down what she says.

a) You will be rich.

b) __________

c) __________

d) __________

e) __________

Aufgabe 2 Translate.

a) Wird es in der Zukunft genauso viele Kriege geben wie in der Vergangenheit?

b) Wann werden die Menschen endlich lernen, dass sie in Frieden besser leben?

c) Was muss noch geschehen (= wird noch geschehen müssen), damit es endlich alle glauben?

d) Ohne Krieg werden endlich alle Menschen ruhig schlafen.

6.2 *going-to-future*

Wann verwendest du das *going-to-future?*

Du benutzt das *going-to-future*, um **Pläne, Vorhaben, Absichten** zu formulieren.

Beispiel: What are you going to do next week?

Wie bildest du das *going-to-future?*

Form von *to be* + *going to* + Infinitiv des Verbs;
Verneinung: *to be* wird verneint

Beispiele:

I am
you / we / you / they are } going to go
he / she / it is

He isn't going to leave.

Aufgabe 3 Write down what Tom is going to do during the holidays next week.

a) On Monday, he's going to play tennis.

b) ______

c) ______

d) ______

e) ________________________________

f) ________________________________

g) ________________________________

Aufgabe 4 On Sunday, Tom meets Patricia and asks her if she is going to do something with him next week. But she has different plans. Write their dialogue.

a) TOM: Are you going to play tennis with me tomorrow? (tennis)
PATRICIA: No, I'm going to work in my uncle's shop. (work)

b) TOM: ____________________ (picnic)
PATRICIA: ____________________ (visit cousins)

c) TOM: ____________________ (visit a museum)
PATRICIA: ____________________ (play with baby sister)

d) TOM: ____________________ (swimming)
PATRICIA: ____________________ (volleyball)

e) TOM: ____________________ (shopping)
PATRICIA: ____________________ (do work for school)

f) TOM: ____________________ (fly model plane)
PATRICIA: ____________________ (bicycle tour)

g) TOM: ____________________ (stay in bed)
PATRICIA: ____________________ (TV)

6.3 *present progressive* und *simple present* zum Ausdruck von Zukunft

Wann verwendest du *present progressive* und *simple present* zum Ausdruck von Zukunft?

In manchen Fällen kannst du auch die englischen Gegenwartszeiten verwenden, um über zukünftige Handlungen zu sprechen.

- Für **bereits getroffene Vereinbarungen, Pläne** und **Vorhaben** kannst du das *present progressive* benutzen, jedoch nur, wenn klar ist, dass es im Satz um die Zukunft geht (z. B. durch entsprechende Adverbien).

  Beispiel: We're visiting our friends next week, you know, and Susan is coming with us.

- Ist das **zukünftige Geschehen bereits im Voraus festgelegt** (z. B. Fahrplan, Termine), kannst du auch das *simple present* gebrauchen. Aber auch hier muss klar sein, dass es um die Zukunft geht.

  Beispiel: Our train leaves at 9:36 on Monday morning.

Aufgabe 5 Put in the right tenses to express future.

SUSAN: When ____________[1] (your parents, come) back?

PETER: They write that they ____________[2] (be) back home on Wednesday afternoon, but I know there ____________[3] (be) no train at that time next Wednesday because it's a holiday. I ____________[4] (have to) ring them up again and tell them.

SUSAN: Well, what about a bike tour on Tuesday then? ____________[5] (you, go) with me?

PETER: No, I can't. Our cleaning lady is on holiday, and so I ____________[6] (clean) all the house on Tuesday. And then, school ____________[7] (start) again next week, and I don't want to be in trouble again, so I ____________[8] (work) a lot for school, even in the holidays.

SUSAN: Really? What ____________[9] (you, do)?

PETER: I've already started maths, and tomorrow I ____________[10] (learn) my German words.

SUSAN: O dear! So we ____________[11] (not do) anything together this week?

PETER: I'm afraid not!

Aufgabe 6 Complete the travellers' dialogues. Use *present progressive* or *simple present.*

Tipps zum Artikulieren der eigenen Meinung in einem *short essay*

Im Englischunterricht bist du sicher schon oft nach deiner Meinung zu einem bestimmten Thema gefragt worden. Deine Meinung konntest du dann in wenigen Sätzen begründen. Wenn du aber dazu aufgefordert wirst, deine Meinung in einem ***short essay*** zum Ausdruck zu bringen, solltest du ein paar formale Dinge besonders beachten:

- Schreibe einen kleinen **Aufsatz**, also einen Text mit **Einleitung**, **Hauptteil** und **Schluss**.
- Leg dir im Kopf oder auf einem **Konzeptblatt** zurecht, was du schreiben willst, bevor du mit dem Schreiben beginnst.
- **In der kurzen Einleitung** solltest du bereits eindeutig **Stellung beziehen**. Am Anfang könnte z. B. stehen: *In my opinion; As to me; Personally, I do not think …*
- Deine **Meinung** musst du **im Hauptteil** mit mindestens drei guten Argumenten **untermauern**. Wenn du genügend Zeit und Ideen hast, kannst du natürlich auch noch ein Gegenargument bringen und es danach entkräften. Für ‚zwar – aber' verwendet man im Englischen *It is true – but.*
- **Im Schlussteil** kannst du kurz das **Ergebnis deines Nachdenkens wiederholen**, z. B. indem du schreibst: *This is why I think …; This is why I believe …*
- **Verbinde deine Sätze** miteinander. Neben den üblichen Konjunktionen (z. B. *but, yet, after all*) solltest du auch deine Argumente ‚durchzählen' (z. B. *firstly, secondly, finally*).

ufgabe 7* Your opinion

You have certainly seen some (or all?) episodes of *Star Trek* or *Star Wars* or similar science fiction films. What do you think: Is this what the future will be like? Write down your ideas in a short essay of about eight sentences.

7 Konditional und Bedingungssätze

Um anderen mitzuteilen, „was gewesen wäre, wenn ...“ oder „was sein würde, wenn ...“, musst du **Bedingungssätze** bilden. Im Englischen stehen die Verben, die du zur Bildung solcher Sätze brauchst, im **Konditional**. Im Deutschen steht hier der Konjunktiv.

7.1 *conditional* und *conditional perfect*

Wann verwendest du das *conditional*?

Um auszudrücken, was unter bestimmten Umständen **geschehen würde**, verwendest du das *conditional*.

Beispiel: In that case, I wouldn't go.

Das *conditional* kannst du auch als ***future of the past*** in der **indirekten Rede** verwenden. In einem solchen Fall musst du, bei einem einleitenden Satz in der Vergangenheit, das *will-future* der wörtlichen Rede in *conditional* in der indirekten Rede umwandeln (siehe auch S. 155).

Beispiel: She thought, "They will arrive on time."
She thought they would arrive on time.

Wie bildest du das *conditional*?

would (could) + Infinitiv; Verneinung: *wouldn't (couldn't)* + Infinitiv

Beispiel: leave → would leave

Aufgabe 1 What would Pete do with $ 1 million? Write down his ideas.

a)

I would buy a big house.

____

b)

TICKET
WORLD
TOUR

____

____

c)

Thank you, grandpa!

____

____

d)

NO
Back to work!
BOSS

____

____

e)

NEW YORK

We ______________________________

____

f)

g)

h)

We

Wann verwendest du das *conditional perfect?*

Um auszudrücken, was unter bestimmten Umständen **geschehen wäre**, benutzt du das *conditional perfect.*

Beispiel: She would have liked to thank me, but it wasn't possible.

Das *conditional perfect* kannst du auch als ***future perfect of the past*** in der **indirekten Rede** verwenden. In einem solchen Fall musst du, bei einem einleitenden Satz in der Vergangenheit, das *future perfect* der wörtlichen Rede in *conditional perfect* in der indirekten Rede umwandeln (siehe auch S. 155).

Beispiel: I asked her, "Will you have finished by ten?"
I asked her if she would have finished by ten.

Wie bildest du das *conditional perfect?*

would/could + have + past participle;
Verneinung: *wouldn't/couldn't + have + past participle*
Beispiel: drive → would have driven

Aufgabe 2 Imagine you had bad weather yesterday. With a lot of sunshine, what would you have done? The pictures will help you.

a) I would have gone swimming.

b) ______________________________

c) ______________________________

d) ______________________________

e) ______________________________

f) ______________________________

ufgabe 3 The Randolphs have never had $ 1 million, but what if …? Write down what they would have done (a – d) and what they would not have done (e – h). Use the pictures in exercise 1 for your sentences.

a) They would have bought a big house.

b) ______

c) ______

d) ______

e) ______

f) ______

g) ______

h) ______

Tipps für das Schreiben von formellen E-Mails

Eine E-Mail an einen Freund oder Bekannten darf außergewöhnlich aussehen und salopp geschrieben sein, doch beim Schreiben formeller E-Mails solltest du ein paar Regeln beachten:

- Verwende wie beim förmlichen Brief eine **förmliche Anrede** (*Dear Sirs,*) und eine entsprechende **Schlussformel** (*Yours sincerely,*).
- Die Anrede endet mit Komma, der Text in der nächsten Zeile beginnt mit einem Großbuchstaben.
- Die formelle E-Mail sollte **höflich verfasst** sein (z. B. *Could you please, …; I would like to ask you to …; Would you be so kind as to …*).
- Vergiss nicht, dich am Ende zu **bedanken** (z. B. *Thank you very much for your trouble; Thank you very much in advance*).

ufgabe 4* You want to spend your holidays in Great Britain. Take a map of the British Isles to choose a town or region, and then write an e-mail to the local Tourist Board to get some information. Write about four sentences. (You can look for addresses on the Internet via any search engine and then send this e-mail for real; I'm sure you will get a positive answer!)

7.2 Bedingungssätze

Was sind Bedingungssätze?

Bedingungssätze (*conditional sentences*) sind Satzgefüge, die aus zwei Satzteilen bestehen: dem **konditionalen Gliedsatz (if-Satz)**, in dem die Bedingung steht, und dem **Hauptsatz** (*main clause*), der die Folgerung enthält, die sich ergibt, wenn die genannte Bedingung erfüllt oder nicht erfüllt wird.

Grundsätzlich unterscheidet man Bedingungen, die objektiv **erfüllbar** oder **nicht erfüllbar** sind, bzw. die der Sprecher für erfüllbar oder nicht erfüllbar hält.

Beispiele: If Robin goes to Nottingham, he will have to go in disguise.
If he hadn't robbed the rich, he wouldn't have been able to give money to the poor.

Wie bildest du Bedingungssätze?

- **Typ 1: Erfüllbare Bedingung**
  Im *if*-Satz steht eine Bedingung, die erfüllt werden kann, da sich der Satz auf die Zukunft bezieht.
  if-Satz: *simple present*; Hauptsatz: *will-future*

  Beispiel: If the Sheriff of Nottingham <u>catches</u> Robin, he <u>will hang</u> him.

  Bei diesen erfüllbaren Bedingungen kann im Hauptsatz auch das Präsens stehen. Der Sprecher möchte dann ausdrücken, dass unter den gleichen Bedingungen immer wieder das gleiche Ergebnis eintritt. Mit diesen Sätzen kannst du also **allgemeingültige Wahrheiten** ausdrücken.
  if-Satz: *simple present;* Hauptsatz: *simple present*

  Beispiel: If you <u>need</u> help, you <u>needn't ask</u> the rich.

- **Typ 2 a: Unwahrscheinliche Bedingung**
  Im *if*-Satz steht eine Bedingung, die erfüllt werden kann, da sie sich auf die Gegenwart oder die Zukunft bezieht. Allerdings erscheint die Erfüllung der Bedingung eher unwahrscheinlich.

  if-Satz: *simple past;* Hauptsatz: *conditional*

  Beispiel: If Robin's men <u>left</u> him, he <u>wouldn't be able</u> to help the poor any more.

- **Typ 2 b: Nicht erfüllbare Bedingung**
  Im *if*-Satz steht eine Bedingung, die nicht erfüllt werden kann, obwohl sich die Bedingung auf die Gegenwart bezieht.

  if-Satz: *simple past;* Hauptsatz: *conditional*

  Beispiel: If I were an outlaw, I would try to be like Robin Hood.
- **Typ 3: Nicht erfüllbare Bedingung**
  Im *if*-Satz steht eine Bedingung, die nicht mehr erfüllt werden kann, da sie sich auf die **Vergangenheit** bezieht. Somit stellt der Satz eine bloße Annahme, ein Gedankenspiel dar.

  if-Satz: *past perfect;* Hauptsatz: *conditional perfect*

  Beispiel: If the situation in England hadn't been so bad, Robin wouldn't have become the helper of the poor.

Der *if*-Satz kann vor wie nach dem Hauptsatz stehen. Steht der *if*-Satz vor dem Hauptsatz, wird ein Komma eingefügt.

Beispiel: If the outlaws hadn't hidden well, the Sheriff would have caught them.
The Sheriff would have caught the outlaws if they hadn't hidden well.

ufgabe 5 Complete the chain of ifs. Be careful with the tenses.

a) If there's no school tomorrow, I *will stay* at home all day.

b) If I stay at home all day, my friends ____________ come early.

c) If my friends ____________, we ____________ play longer than usual.

d) If we ____________, the day ____________ be much nicer.

e) If the day ____________, I ____________ be happier.

f) If I ____________, my parents and I ____________ not quarrel so much.

g) If we ____________, they ____________ let me go to the cinema.

h) If they ____________, I ____________ at last see that great film.

i) If I ____________, I ____________ to talk about it with my classmates.

Aufgabe 6 Complete the chain of ifs. Use the sentences in exercise 5. Be careful with the tenses.

a) If there were no school today, I would stay at home all day.

b) If I stayed at home all day, my friends ____________________

c) ____________________

d) ____________________

e) ____________________

f) ____________________

g) ____________________

h) ____________________

i) ____________________

Aufgabe 7 Complete the chain of ifs. Use the sentences in exercise 5. Be careful with the tenses.

a) If there had been no school yesterday, I would have stayed at home all day.

b) If I had stayed at home all day, my friends ____________________

c) ____________________

d) ____________________

e) ____________________

f) ____________________

g) ____________________

h) ____________________

i) ____________________

Aufgabe 8 Fill in the correct tenses.

Pit and Lea are standing in front of the cinema.

PIT: If you go to see that film, I ____________________[1] (not go) with you.
LEA: Why not? If I ____________________[2] (know) that, I wouldn't have asked you.
PIT: I'll tell you why. If you ____________________[3] (watch) that film, you will cry all the time; it's so sad, and I don't like to see you crying. If I didn't mind seeing you crying, I ____________________[4] (go) with you.
LEA: Well, what else can we do then? How about another film? If there ____________________[5] (be) another film which were not so sad, would you watch it with me?
PIT: Of course. But there is none. If they showed another one, I ____________________[6] (know) about it.
LEA: It seems to me it ____________________[7] (be) better if we had stayed at home.
PIT: Okay, let's go home then. Bye, Lea.
LEA: Bye, Pit. If you want to meet me again, you ____________________[8] (have to) have a good idea!

Aufgabe 9 Fill in the right tenses.

Mr and Mrs Parker are buying clothes for Mr Parker.

MRS PARKER: What about this pink pullover? You've never had a pink one.
MR PARKER: I don't know. Don't you think everybody ____________________[1] (laugh) if I ____________________[2] (wear) a pink pullover?
SHOP ASSISTANT: If you ____________________[3] (not like) the pink one, I'm sure you ____________________[4] (like) this blue one.
MR PARKER: But it's too small.
SHOP ASSISTANT: Well, if this one ____________________[5] (be) too small, you ____________________[6] (have to) take this yellow one.
Mrs Parker: But he doesn't like yellow. If yellow ____________________[7] (be) one of his favourite colours, we ____________________[8] (buy) this pullover at once.
SHOP ASSISTANT: Sorry, if you ____________________[9] (tell) me before, I ____________________[10] (not show) you that yellow pullover.

MR PARKER: Haven't you got something like the grey pullover in the window? You know, if we ________________[11] (not see) that one, we ________________[12] (not come) in at all.

SHOP ASSISTANT: [thinks] If I ____________[13] (not find) a suitable pullover soon, they ________________[14] (go) away and not buy anything! [says] Oh yes, of course. If I ________________[15] (think) of that one, I'm sure we ________________[16] (find) the right one for you already.

MRS PARKER: [to Mr Parker] If this one ________________[17] (not be) exactly what we want, we ________________[18] (leave), ________________[19] we?

MR PARKER: Yes, of course. It seems they haven't got many nice pullovers in my size. If they ________________[20] (have) more, she ________________[21] (certainly show) them to us.

SHOP ASSISTANT: Er, sorry, but we have no more pullovers in your size. I'm afraid you ________________[22] (have to) come again in two weeks' time if you ________________[23] (want) to see our new collection. Goodbye.

MR and MRS PARKER: Goodbye.

Neben den drei Haupttypen von Bedingungssätzen solltest du noch über zwei weitere Typen Bescheid wissen:

- **Mischtyp aus 2 und 3:**
  Im *if*-Satz steht eine immer gültige Bedingung, der Hauptsatz bezieht sich auf die Vergangenheit.
  if-Satz: *simple past*; Hauptsatz: *conditional perfect*
  Beispiel: If the British didn't like people who stand up against authorities, Robin Hood wouldn't have become a folk hero.
- **Mischtyp aus 3 und 2:**
  Im *if*-Satz steht eine Bedingung, die nicht mehr erfüllt werden kann, der Hauptsatz bezieht sich aber auf die Gegenwart, in der die Folge zu spüren ist.
  if-Satz: *past perfect*; Hauptsatz: *conditional*
  Beispiel: If Robin Hood hadn't become an outlaw, he wouldn't be the most famous British folk hero today.

- Das **deutsche ‚wenn'** kann zwei verschiedene Bedeutungen haben: **zeitlich** (‚wenn', ‚sobald') entspricht es dem englischen *when* und **konditional** (‚wenn', ‚falls') entspricht es dem englischen *if*.

  Beispiel: When you are in Rome, will you call me? (wenn, sobald)
  If you go to New York, will you write me a letter? (falls)

gabe 10* What if …? Match the right pairs of clauses and put in the correct tenses.

a) Thomas Alva Edison (not invent) the light bulb …
b) John D. Rockefeller (not make) so much money …
c) The Wright Brothers (give up) after their first attempts …
d) We (have) no electricity …
e) He (not know) that he would make a lot of money with it …
f) Life today (be) much easier than life in the past …
g) Printers (not start) to introduce typewriters in the 1880s …
h) Henry Ford (not produce) his model T on the assembly line …

(1) … all the inventors' efforts (be) in vain.
(2) … perhaps modern planes (not exist).
(3) … Elias Howe (not try) to invent a sewing-machine.
(4) … we (have to) go to bed much earlier.
(5) … he (not sell) thousands of cars in a few months.
(6) … it (be) certainly because of all the good ideas some people have had.
(7) … the development of computers (not become) possible.
(8) … the Rockefeller Foundation (not can) help so many gifted people since it was founded.

a 4: If T. A. Edison hadn't invented the light bulb, we would have to go to bed much earlier.

Aufgabe 11* Did you know all these things about Manhattan? Make conditional sentences with the information in the following sentences.

a) Manhattan could only be built as it was because people had $ 24 to buy the island from the Indians.

If people hadn't had $ 24 to buy the island from the Indians, New York couldn't have been built as it was.

b) Manhattan is so big that you can't walk from its northern end to its southern end.

c) The skyscrapers are so high that you can never see the sun in some streets.

d) The Empire State Building is higher than the Chrysler Building, so it is the highest skyscraper in Manhattan.

e) Architects are always looking for space in Manhattan to build houses in.

f) But there is very little space; so architects who want to build new skyscrapers are ready to tear down old ones.

g) Today Manhattan is mostly famous for its skyline.

h) The streets in Manhattan were laid out like a chessboard because one mayor decided this would make the island more attractive.

i) Central Park is the only place in Manhattan where its inhabitants can breathe fresh air.

fgabe 12 Translate.

a) Wenn Robin Hood und seine Männer nicht immer verkleidet gewesen wären, hätte der Sheriff von Nottingham sie sofort erkannt.

b) Wenn ihre Kleidung alt und zerrissen war, gingen sie auf den Markt in Lincoln.

c) Robin sagte immer: „Wenn ihr noch etwas anderes findet, könnt ihr es auch kaufen.“

d) Oft antworteten seine Männer: „In Ordnung, wenn wir noch etwas sehen, kaufen wir es.

e) Aber wenn wir mehr Geld hätten, könnten wir noch mehr kaufen.

f) Wir hätten mehr Geld, wenn du uns erlaubt hättest, noch mehr Reiche auszurauben."

g) „Das glaube ich nicht", pflegte Robin zu antworten, „denn wenn wir mehr Geld hätten, hättet ihr es schon längst ausgegeben.

h) Wisst ihr: Wenn ihr etwas Schönes seht, wollt ihr es immer gleich haben.

i) Und außerdem (= Und dann) dürft ihr nicht vergessen: Wenn wir die Reichen ausraubten, um das Geld für uns zu verwenden, wären wir keine Gesetzlosen, sondern einfache Diebe!"

8 Passiv

Während ein Aktivsatz Auskunft darüber gibt, wer oder was etwas tut, stellt ein **Passivsatz** die **Person** oder **Sache in den Mittelpunkt** des Interesses, **mit der etwas geschieht**.

Beispiel: People throw away all sorts of things. *(active)*
All sorts of things are thrown away. *(passive)*

8.1 Zeitformen des Passivs

Wann verwendest du das Passiv?

- Du verwendest das Passiv *(passive)*, wenn **nicht so wichtig ist oder du nicht weißt, wer etwas tut, getan hat oder tun wird**.

  Beispiel: The earth is being destroyed more and more.

- Auch wenn du **stärker betonen möchtest, was passiert, passiert ist oder passieren wird**, als wer es tut, getan hat oder tun wird, kannst du das Passiv verwenden.

  Beispiel: The air is polluted.

- Da beim Passiv der Urheber der Handlung nicht genannt werden muss, wird es auch gerne verwendet, um **offizielle Texte**, also Artikel, Zeitungsmeldungen, Geschäftsbriefe etc., **objektiv** erscheinen zu lassen.

  Beispiel: Laws have to be made so that pollution can be prevented.

- Das Passiv kannst du auch einsetzen, wenn du in einem Satz das zuletzt genannte Element des vorausgegangenen Satzes als Subjekt wieder aufnehmen willst.

  Beispiel: We need <u>clean air</u>, but <u>it</u> cannot be easily cleaned.

Rund um die *simple*-Formen des Passivs

Wie bildest du die *simple*-Formen des Passivs?

- Du bildest die *simple*-Formen des Passivs mit einer **Form von *to be*** und dem ***past participle***.

  Beispiel: A lot of oil is wasted.

- Du kannst im Englischen Passivsätze mit beinahe allen Verben bilden. Voraussetzung ist nur, dass sie im Aktivsatz ein Objekt haben. Denn das **Objekt des Aktivsatzes**, also die Person oder Sache, mit der etwas geschieht, wird zum **Subjekt des Passivsatzes** (siehe dazu S. 97).

  Beispiel: Smoke fills the air. *(active)*
  The air is filled with smoke. *(passive)*

Die folgende Tabelle zeigt dir das Aktiv und Passiv in verschiedenen Zeiten der *simple*-Form. Lerne diese Tabelle auswendig!

tense	*active*	*passive*
simple pres.	Man pollutes the air.	The air is polluted.
simple past	Man polluted the air.	The air was polluted.
present perf.	Man has polluted the air.	The air has been polluted.
past perfect	Man had polluted the air.	The air had been polluted.
future	Man will pollute the air.	The air will be polluted.
conditional	Man would pollute the air.	The air would be polluted.
future perf.	Man will have polluted the air.	The air will have been polluted.
condi. perf.	Man would have polluted the air.	The air would have been polluted.
auxiliary + infinitive	Man can pollute the air.	The air can be polluted.
gerund/participle	Man polluting the air …	The air being polluted …

ufgabe 1 Cars sometimes come to a standstill – when they are out of order. Say what is done at a garage.

a) *The tank is filled up.* ______________________

b) ______________________

c) ______________________

d) ______________________

e) ______________________

f) ______________________

g) ______________________

h) ______________________

ufgabe 2 When Jack was going through the city centre yesterday, a lot of things happened. Make sentences in the *passive*, using the following verbs:
fell, close, throw, mow, drop, lift.

a) A bottle ______________________ on Jack's head.

b) Stones ______________________ at him.

c) A tree ______________________ in a garden.

d) A car ______________________ out of the river.

e) The grass in the park ______________________.

f) A greengrocer's ______________________ the moment he came.

Rund um die *progressive*-Formen des Passivs

Wann verwendest du die *progressive*-Formen des Passivs?

Die *progressive*-Formen betonen im Passiv ganz besonders, dass etwas gerade passiert bzw. zu einem bestimmten Zeitpunkt geschah oder geschehen wird.

Beispiel: Hundreds of trees are being felled this minute.

Wie bildest du die *progressive*-Formen des Passivs?

- Du bildest die *progressive*-Formen des Passiv mit einer **Form von *to be***, dem Wort ***being*** und dem ***past participle***.

  Beispiel: Nothing is being done about it.

- Auch im *progressive* wird das Objekt des Aktivsatzes zum Subjekt des Passivsatzes.

  Beispiel: We are constantly polluting the air.
  The air is constantly being polluted.

Die *progressive*-Form wird im Passiv in der Regel nur im *present* und im *past tense* verwendet.

	active	*passive*
present prog.	They are making new laws.	New laws are being made.
past prog.	They were making new laws.	New laws were being made.

Aufgabe 3 Look at the picture in exercise 1 again. Now make sentences of the following type:

a) When I arrived *at the filling-station, the tank of my car was just being filled up.*

b) When I arrived ______

c) ______

d) ______

e) ______

f) ______

g) ______

h) ______

ufgabe 4 Translate, using the passive for the German construction with 'man' or 'jemand'.

a) Jemand verschmutzt seit Tagen den Fluss.

____

b) Man musste ihn säubern.

____

c) Alle hoffen, dass irgendjemand die Polizei informieren wird.

____

d) Man sucht gerade nach dem Verbrecher.

____

e) Man hat ihn noch nicht gefunden.

____

f) Keiner weiß, ob man ihn wirklich fassen wird.

____

ufgabe 5 Read the following text and answer the questions on it.

When asked about their cars, many people all over the world first of all talk about its performance: horsepower, top speed, acceleration, ... Only rarely can you hear answers like, "I'm glad it runs on 6 litres per 100 km" or "It's the most silent car in our street." Cars are still widely seen as an object of prestige: the faster your car goes, the more your friends and neighbours will be impressed.

Yet, everybody ought to know by now that cars pollute the environment, that roads and motorways which have to be built for them destroy nature and that the noise of cars is often intolerable for people who live along busy streets. The biggest problem at present is that carbon monoxide and other poisonous substances in the exhaust fumes of cars still play an important part in the destruction of the ozone layer and the greenhouse effect. Catalytic converters and less gas-guzzling cars have helped to reduce the problem, but this alone cannot solve it.

Three strategies can lead to a positive change. On the one hand, technical progress is needed. The less petrol a car needs, the less poisonous its exhaust fumes will be. It is high time the automobile industry developed less thirsty cars and less poisonous petrol. But, on the other hand, the users of cars will have to adapt, too. They will have to be ready to pay a higher price for a new, better car and for better petrol, and they ought to think twice before they use their car. Many people still go by car even though they could just as well walk or go by bus or train. And this, finally, is the third change necessary: public transport must be made even more attractive, we need more, and faster and more reliable, buses, trams and trains, to make it easier – both for businessmen and for families with children – to leave their car in the garage and be driven to their destination instead of driving there themselves.

a) Find a suitable title for this text.
b) The three paragraphs of the text talk about three different aspects of the problem. Give a summary of the text by first writing in one sentence what the whole text is about, and then writing one or two sentences about each of the three paragraphs.
   Use your own words as far as possible.
c) What, according to the first paragraph, should be important for an environment-conscious car driver?
d) What negative effects does car driving have on the environment?
e) In how far are catalytic converters and less gas-guzzling cars environmentally friendly?
f) According to the last paragraph, how will people's behaviour have to change?
g) Find the passive forms in the text and turn the sentences with them into active voice. There are seven of them.

8.2 Der Passivsatz

Rund um den *by-agent*

- Wenn du im Passivsatz doch sagen möchtest, wer oder was etwas tut, getan hat oder tun wird, so kannst du den **Initiator des Geschehens mit *by*** anschließen (*by-agent*). Dadurch wird er besonders betont.

  Beispiel: The air is mainly polluted by cars, but also by factories.

- Wenn du einen Aktivsatz in einen Passivsatz umwandeln willst, wird das **Subjekt des Aktivsatzes zum *by-agent*** – oder, wenn möglich, weggelassen –, das **Objekt des Aktivsatzes** wird zum **Subjekt des Passivsatzes** und das Verb wird umgeformt.

  Beispiel: Each of us pollutes our water. } *active*

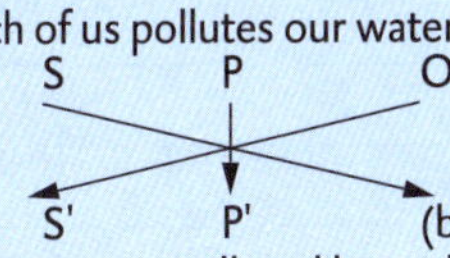

  Our water is polluted by each of us. } *passive*

ufgabe 6 Turn the following sentences into the passive voice. Decide whether the agent must be mentioned or not. There might be more than one passive in a sentence.

Many car drivers do not give a thought to the pollution which the burning of their cars' fuel might cause. In addition, every minute, factories are letting tons of dirt into the rivers and a lot of smoke into the air. Most of the things which man produces and which we need in everyday life might pollute the air or the water. We can find the traces which cars, central heating and plastic bags leave everywhere. On the other hand, we can read and hear a lot about pollution and its effects. We know today that we need new ideas. But is somebody already producing better systems? Are we fighting the pollution of the seas, lakes and rivers? Man must develop new ideas if he doesn't want to destroy the world completely. One example are new plastic bags: it's easy to burn them. If man doesn't help nature, it is certain to die.

No thought is given by many car drivers to the pollution which might be caused by the burning of their cars' fuel.

Aufgabe 7* Complete the following information about litter and recycling in Great Britain with verbs in the passive, so that it really sounds like an official text.

Litter mustn't ______________[1] (leave) in any outdoor public place. The maximum penalty ______________[2] (raise) in 1992 to £ 2,500. To help solve the problem of litter, money – all in all £ 2.9 million in 1994 – ______________[3] (give) to the Tidy Britain Group, which ______________[4] (recognise) as the national agency for preventing littering. The recycling of waste materials ______________[5] (practise) by the Government whenever this is practicable. It hopes that half of all recyclable household waste ______________[6] (recycle) by 2000. Plans have to ______________[7] (make) in every town for the recycling of waste. Used glass containers can ______________[8] (throw) into bottle banks for recycling. Nearly 15,000 such banks ______________[9] (put up) in Britain, and over 1,000 can banks. In addition, waste material ______________[10] (collect) by voluntary organisations.

Rund um das Passiv bei Verben mit präpositionalem Objekt

Wenn du einen Aktivsatz mit einem präpositionalen Objekt *(prepositional object)* in einen Passivsatz umwandelst, darfst du auch **im Passivsatz die Präposition nicht vom Verb trennen**.

Beispiel: We must take care of our environment. *(active)*
Our environment must be taken care of. *(passive)*

Lerne die folgenden Beispiele für Verben und Ausdrücke mit Präpositionen auswendig:

to be afraid of	fürchten
to be angry at	wütend sein über
to believe in	glauben an
to choose from	auswählen aus
to give up	aufgeben
to be happy about	froh sein über
to be keen on	gerne tun
to laugh at	lachen über
to listen to	zuhören
to look at/for/after/forward to	anschauen/suchen/sich kümmern um/sich freuen auf
to speak to/about	sprechen mit/über
to talk to/about	sprechen mit/über

Aufgabe 8 Make sentences in the passive. Don't forget to use the right preposition.

a) nature/not always/take care

____

b) environmental problems/not easily/cope

____

c) new ideas/constantly/talk

____

d) warners/sometimes/laugh

____

e) environmentalists/not always/listen

____

Rund um Verben mit direktem und indirektem Objekt

- Wenn du einen Aktivsatz, der sowohl ein direktes als auch ein indirektes Objekt *(direct, indirect object)* hat, ins Passiv umwandelst, können **beide Objekte Subjekt des Passivsatzes** werden. Meist aber wird die Person (indirektes Objekt) zum Subjekt des Passivsatzes (persönliches Passiv).

  Beispiel: Do they always tell everybody the truth? (Aktiv)
  Is everybody always told the truth? (persönliches Passiv)
  Is the truth always told to everybody? (Passiv)

  Folgende Verben haben oft zwei Objekte nach sich: *to allow s.b. sth., to bring s.b. sth., to give s.b. sth., to hand s.b. sth., to leave s.b. sth., to offer s.b. sth., to pay s.b. sth., to sell s.b. sth., to send s.b. sth., to show s.b. sth., to teach s.b. sth., to tell s.b. sth., to write s.b. sth.*

- Manche **Verben** mit zwei Objekten schließen das **indirekte Objekt** immer **mit to** an, z. B. *to announce, to describe, to distribute, to explain, to introduce, to say.* Bei diesen Verben kannst du **nur das direkte Objekt zum Subjekt** des Passivsatzes machen.

  Beispiel: Often, people have announced progress to the population when there was none.
  Often, progress has been announced to the population when there was none.

Aufgabe 9 Look at the pictures and describe what has happened in three ways: active, passive, personal passive. You will see that in all cases personal passive is best.

a)

Linda – write – letter

A letter has been written to Linda.

Somebody has written Linda a letter.

Linda has been written a letter.

b)

Rosie – hand – newspaper

____

____

____

c) 

the Clarks – sell – house

d) 

Billy – give some extra homework

e) 

Mr Riley – offer – a cheap car

f) 

Milly – teach – song

Aufgabe 10 Mr Miller comes back to his home town after ten years and talks to Mr Snider about what has changed. Complete the dialogue; use passive voice.

MR MILLER: What has happened to all the trees?
MR SNIDER: They ______________________________ [1].
MR MILLER: There are more houses now, aren't there?
MR SNIDER: Yes, they ______________________________ [2] in 1988.
MR MILLER: But the park is still the same size, isn't it?
MR SNIDER: Yes, its size ______________________________ [3].
MR MILLER: The lake in it is new, though, isn't it?
MR SNIDER: It ______________________________ [4] two or three years ago.
MR MILLER: Do you see those road sweepers? Just like in the good old days!
MR SNIDER: Yes, their job ______________________________ [5] just like it was ten years ago.

gabe 11* Turn the following sentences into the active voice. Put in suitable subjects where necessary. There might be more than one active in a sentence!

When the first cars were being driven through the London streets, a law was made by Parliament saying that pedestrians and horse coaches had to be warned by a man with a red flag. In some American towns, the speed limit was fixed at 10 miles per hour. New York was the first city whose policemen were offered bicycles so that cars driving too fast could be caught. Today, such stories can only be laughed at. And in future? Will cars be replaced by something new? And how much will this new thing be feared in the beginning?

Aufgabe 12* First read the following text. Then answer the questions in two ways: with an active and a passive sentence.

Some of the pioneers in the wild west were early environmentalists, like Natty Bumppo "Leatherstocking" in James Fenimore Cooper's novels in the 1820's, 1830's and 1840's. He was based on the model of one of the real pioneers, Daniel Boone.
Leatherstocking is everything that any American boy ever dreamed of being. He was fearless and able to do everything, shot fantastically and was the most loyal of friends. As a frontiersman, a pioneer, he felt obliged to be on the side of civilization; but civilization was at war with the wilderness, which he loved. So the carriers of civilization in Cooper's books, the settlers, are often the bad characters, they destroy the beauty and liberty of the woods.
The same townsmen who throw Natty Bumppo into jail for shooting a deer out of season, fire into a flock of passenger pigeons with every weapon in town, even a cannon.
Wilderness man cannot live with settlement man. Like Daniel Boone, when he feels too many people nearby, Natty goes on west, and Cooper's sympathy as well as the reader's goes with him.

a) What second name did Cooper give Natty Bumppo in his novels?
Cooper gave Natty Bumppo the name Leatherstocking.
Natty Bumppo was given the name Leatherstocking (by Cooper).

b) When did Cooper write his "Leatherstocking" novels?

____

c) Who did Cooper use as his model for Leatherstocking?

____

____

d) On what terms were civilization and wilderness at that time?

____

____

e) What did the settlers do to the beauty and liberty of the woods?

____

____

f) Why did the townsmen throw Natty Bumppo into jail?

____

____

g) What often happened to passenger pigeons in that town?

____

____

Tipps zur Bildbeschreibung

Wenn du ein Bild beschreiben sollst, musst du ein paar Dinge beachten:

- **Sieh** dir **das Bild** zunächst ganz **genau an**.
- Der **Titel** kann dir dabei helfen, dich ein wenig in die Situation hineinzuversetzen, die gemalt oder fotografiert wurde.
- **Beginne** deine Beschreibung **mit einem allgemeinen Satz über das Bild** und sage dabei, um was für eine Art Bild es sich handelt (*photo, painting, landscape, portrait, war scene* etc.).
- **Beschreibe so genau wie möglich**; halte dabei eine **sinnvolle Reihenfolge** ein und springe nicht ständig zwischen verschiedenen Bildteilen hin und her.
- Bei einem Bild wirst du niemals alles sicher wissen; du darfst in deine Beschreibung daher durchaus auch **Spekulationen aufnehmen** (*perhaps; might; I think; it looks as if; apparently; it seems to; …*).

ufgabe 13* Have a look at the picture in exercise 12 (p. 104) again. Describe the picture and give it a suitable title.

9 Infinitiv

Es gibt in der Grammatik finite und infinite Verbformen. Finite Verbformen erzählen etwas über die grammatische Person, die Zahl und die Zeit. **Infinite Verbformen** enthalten solche Informationen nicht. Zu diesen infiniten Verben gehört neben dem Gerundium und dem Partizip auch der **Infinitiv**.

Der **Infinitiv** kann **mit und ohne *to*** stehen und von allen Verben außer den modalen Hilfsverben gebildet werden. Es gibt den Infinitiv im **Aktiv** und im **Passiv**. Im Satz erfüllt der Infinitiv die unterschiedlichsten Funktionen, da er sowohl **Eigenschaften eines Verbs** als auch die **eines Nomens** besitzt. Er kann u. a. **Objekt, Attribut** und **adverbiale Bestimmung** sein.

Beispiele: The settlers hoped to find good land.
Their hope to find friendly Indians wasn't always fulfilled.
They often went to their camps to talk about peace.

9.1 Infinitiv mit *to*

Wann verwendest du den Infinitiv mit *to*?

- Wie im Deutschen kannst du den **Infinitiv mit *to*** nach vielen **Adjektiven** und **ihren Steigerungsformen** verwenden.

  Beispiele: It wasn't easy to find friendly Indians.
  Many settlers found it easier to fight the Indians.

- Du verwendest den Infinitiv mit *to* auch, um eine **Absicht** oder einen **Zweck** auszudrücken sowie nach bestimmten Ausdrücken, die eine **Folge** beschreiben, z. B. *in order to, so as to, to be designed to, to be used to.*

  Beispiele: The white settlers came to the west to start a new life.
  Pioneers went westward in order to find good land.

- Ebenso kannst du den Infinitiv mit *to* verwenden, um einen Relativsatz zu vermeiden, und zwar nach **Ordnungszahlen**, nach **Superlativen, superlativischen Ausdrücken** und nach ***the only***, nach **Nomen**, nach ***somebody, someone*** usw.

  Beispiele: The pioneers were the first who opened the way to the west.
  The pioneers were the first to open the way to the west.

  The biggest problem they had to solve was how to avoid the Indians.
  Their biggest problem to solve was how to avoid the Indians.

  They needed every single man who could help.
  They needed every single man to help.

  There was nobody who could advise them.
  There was nobody to advise them.

- Um einen Nebensatz mit einem modalen Hilfsverb zu vermeiden, kannst du nach **Fragewörtern** und nach ***whether*** den Infinitiv mit *to* verwenden.

  Beispiele: How should they know what they could do when they met an Indian?
  How should they know what to do when they met an Indian?

  Nobody knew whether they should see them as friends or not.
  Nobody knew whether to see them as friends or not.

Aufgabe 1 The all-round machine. Complete the sentences; use infinitives with to.

This machine was designed ____________[1] (sweep) the street and ____________[2] (water) the garden. It can be used ____________[3] (hang) washing on and ____________[4] (watch) TV on. It's strong enough ____________[5] (pull) heavy vehicles and high enough ____________[6] (serve) as a ladder. It's a machine ____________[7] (paint) buildings and ____________[8] (transport) goods in. It's the best machine ____________[9] (dig) holes with and ____________[10] (cut) grass with. It was built so as ____________[11] (make) little noise and ____________[12] (be) relatively cheap.

Aufgabe 2 The early settlers in North America had to face a lot of problems every day. Would you have been a good pioneer?
Complete the sentences with a suitable verb from the list and a question word: *travel, say, get up, ~~prepare~~, ask, go, do, choose, make, look for.*

Would you know ...

a) how to prepare a good meal without water?

b) ____________ when an Indian talked to you in his language?

c) ____________ something to eat in the forest?

d) ____________ when your horse was ill?

e) ____________ to take care of your things when you went hunting?

f) ____________ herbs ____________ when you needed some medicine?

g) ____________ alone or together with others?

h) ____________ fire?

i) ____________ in the morning without a watch?

j) ____________ when you wanted to go west?

- In einigen Fällen kannst du im Englischen anstelle deutscher dass-Sätze die Konstruktion ***for* + Objekt + Infinitiv mit *to*** verwenden, und zwar **nach unpersönlichen Ausdrücken** wie *it is difficult, it is possible, it is a pity, it is the custom,* **nach Adjektiven mit vorangestelltem *too,* nach Adjektiven mit *enough*** und **nach Verben**, die fest mit *for* verbunden sind (z. B. *to ask for, to wait for, to hope for*).

  Beispiele: It was impossible for the Indians to know what the whites were planning.
  The whites were too strong for the Indians to be able to beat them.
  The whites weren't naive enough for the Indians to defeat them.
  The Indians waited for the whites to leave their land again.

- Nach **Verben des Wünschens** (z. B. *to want, to wish, to prefer, to hate*) und nach **Verben**, die eine **Aufforderung**, einen **Rat** oder eine **Warnung** ausdrücken (z. B. *to ask, to expect, to order, to tell, to warn*), kannst du den Infinitiv mit *to* mit einem eigenen Sinnsubjekt verwenden, das als Nomen oder Personalpronomen in der Objekt-Form vor den Infinitiv mit *to* gestellt wird.

  Beispiele: The Indians didn't want the whites to be their enemies.
  They had expected them to be their friends.

Aufgabe 3 Make sentences, using an infinitive. Be careful with the word order.

a) it/not easy/settlers/get in contact with Indians

___

b) there/lots of opportunities/meet some/them

___

c) but/most settlers/too dangerous/them/go and talk

___

d) of course/not want/Indians/on their land/the whites

___

e) too many whites/Indians/be able to beat

___

f) sometimes/wait/fight against each other/Indian tribes

___

g) some whites/Indians/die/prefer

___

h) easy/kill/Indians/guns

___

ufgabe 4 Whenever new settlers came to Bluff City, the Sheriff told them the rules. Write down what he said, using infinitives.

a) We don't want you to disturb ______________________

b) We expect ______________________

c) It must be possible ______________________

d) We warn ______________________

e) We won't allow ______________________

f) It is the custom ______________________

g) Don't be too haughty ______________________

h) Don't hope ______________________

9.2 Infinitiv ohne *to*

Wann verwendest du den Infinitiv ohne *to*?

- Du verwendest den Infinitiv ohne *to* nach **modalen Hilfsverben** mit Ausnahme von *ought* sowie nach *need* und *dare*, wenn diese als Hilfsverben verwendet werden.

  Beispiele: The Indians couldn't resist the whites.
  None of the whites dared tell the Indians openly that they were enemies.

- Nach **Verben des Wahrnehmens und des Beobachtens**, also z. B. nach *notice, see, hear*, verwendest du den Infinitiv ohne *to*.

  Beispiel: The Indians saw the whites kill their buffalo.

- Nach ***make*** (im Sinne von ‚lassen') und nach ***let*** gebrauchst du den Infinitiv ohne *to*.

  Beispiele: They would have liked to make the whites leave.
  The Indians had let them come into their territory.

Aufgabe 5 Translate. Use infinitives whenever you can. You will see that you will be able to avoid difficult constructions with them.

a) Die Siedler kamen in den Wilden Westen, um ein neues Leben zu beginnen.

____

____

b) Die Städte an der Ostküste waren zu voll, als dass sie ihnen Arbeit und einen Platz zum Leben hätten bieten können.

____

____

c) All die Probleme in den Städten ließen sie nach etwas Neuem suchen und viele dachten: „Wir werden woanders besser leben können."

____

____

d) Keiner von ihnen konnte eine der Sprachen der Indianer sprechen und nur manchmal fanden sie jemanden, der ihnen helfen konnte.

____

____

e) Deshalb wussten sie oft nicht, was sie tun sollten, wenn sie Indianer trafen.

____

____

f) „Das Beste, was ihr tun könnt, ist lächeln", hatte man ihnen gesagt.

____

ufgabe 6 Poor Mr Ingman! A wheel of the Ingmans' wagon has broken, and he hasn't managed to repair it. All his family are angry at him. Complete what they say with the following infinitives: *tell, do, try, follow, go, sit, manage, repair.*

Aufgabe 7 Rewrite the sentences, using infinitives with or without to. In each sentence a word to help you is given in brackets.

a) What names of famous Indians do you remember? (can)
What names of famous Indians can you remember?

b) Probably you have already heard someone who mentioned the name of Sitting Bull. (hear)

c) Sitting Bull was one of the first Indians who became world-famous. (first)

d) The Sioux believed that it would be possible that he led and protected them. (possible)

e) So they chose him as their leader when he was still very young. (want)

f) In the Battle of the Rosebud, Sitting Bull and his warriors forced the government troops to retreat. (make)

g) Nine days later, on June 25, 1876, at the little Big Horn, it soon became clear that General Custer would not be able to defeat Sitting Bull. (impossible)

h) Later in his life, the whites ordered Sitting Bull to live on Standing Rock Reservation. (make)

i) He died in a struggle with the Indian police who didn't want him to leave the reservation, following an invitation to Pine Ridge Reservation. (let)

10 Gerundium

Auch das **Gerundium** *(gerund)* zählt zu den **infiniten Verbformen**, denn es enthält – genau wie der Infinitiv und das Partizip – keine Angaben zur grammatischen Person, zur Zahl und zur Zeit. Die *ing*-Form, so wird das Gerundium auch oft genannt, kann sowohl im Aktiv als auch im Passiv stehen und von jedem englischen Vollverb gebildet werden. Auch die Perfektform des Gerundiums wird häufig verwendet. Die Bildung der *ing*-Form kannst du noch einmal auf S. 47 wiederholen.

10.1 Das Gerundium im Satz

Wann verwendest du das Gerundium?

Weil das Gerundium sowohl Eigenschaften eines Verbs als auch die eines Nomens besitzt, kann es unterschiedliche Funktionen im Satz erfüllen:

- Das Gerundium kann **Subjekt** oder **Teil eines Subjekts** sein.

  Beispiele: Dancing has always been an important part of Indian life.
  Riding a horse is fun.

- Ebenso ist es möglich, dass du das **Gerundium als Objekt** einsetzt, vor allem nach folgenden Verben: *to admit* – ‚zugeben'; *to avoid* – ‚vermeiden'; *to enjoy* – ‚sich erfreuen an'; *to finish* – ‚beenden'; *to give up* – ‚aufgeben'; *to go on* – ‚weitermachen'; *to imagine* – ‚sich vorstellen'; *to keep* – ‚weitermachen'; *to mind* – ‚sich stören an'; *to miss* – ‚vermissen'.

  Beispiel: At one point the Indians gave up being friendly to the whites.

  Beachte, dass das Gerundium als Objekt nach *to need* und *to want* passivischen Sinn hat.

  Beispiel: Today, the Indians' rights need defending.
  … müssen verteidigt werden.

- Auch als Teil einer **adverbialen Bestimmung** (z. B. nach den Präpositionen *after, before, by, instead of*) und als **Attribut** kannst du das Gerundium benutzen.

  Beispiele: Instead of leaving the Indians alone, the whites fought them.
  The pioneers had a lot of difficulty in finding their way through the wilderness.

- Nach folgenden Ausdrücken musst du ebenfalls das Gerundium verwenden: *it's no use, it's no good, it's worth (while), I can't help, to be worth, to be busy, What about ...?, How about ...?.*

  Beispiel: Old ghost towns are worth visiting.

- Die Perfektform des Gerundiums kannst du gebrauchen, um **Vorzeitigkeit** auszudrücken.

  Beispiel: After leaving/Having left Plymouth, the Pilgrim Fathers set sail for the New World.

Aufgabe 1 The early European settlers brought all their beliefs and superstitions with them to the New World. Here are some of them. Complete the sentences. Don't forget to use gerunds.

a) 

Throwing ________ a coin into a well is lucky.

b) 

________________ on wood means that nothing bad can happen to you.

c) 

________________ a baby's hair means bad luck.

d) 

What about ________________ a black cat? Well, it means ________________

e) 

It's no use ________________ back!

f) 

________________ a mirror brings you seven years of bad luck.

g) 

It's worth while ____________ with your right foot first.

Aufgabe 2 The early settlers' difficult life. Put in gerunds.

Most of the settlers started ______________________ [1] (travel) to the West because they had to give up ______________________ [2] (find) a good job in the East. Only a few preferred ______________________ [3] (stay) at the east coast. I am sure that nobody enjoyed ______________________ [4] (live) in a waggon for weeks. Most people today prefer ______________________ [5] (stay) in one place, some even for their whole lives. Can you imagine ______________________ [6] (spend) months 'on the road'? Often the waggons broke down and needed ______________________ [7] (repair). Food was not only needed for the people; the horses, too, wanted ______________________ [8] (care) for. In the evenings, the women had to begin ______________________ [9] (work), and I don't think they liked ______________________ [10] (cook) after a long day's journey very much. But they all kept ______________________ [11] (look) for a better place to live, and they didn't mind ______________________ [12] (have) to live a poor and dangerous life. In the day, they tried to avoid ______________________ [13] (meet) Indians, and at night, they loved ______________________ [14] (stay) in a safe place. But of course, nobody would admit ______________________ [15] (be) afraid of anything!

Aufgabe 3 Rewrite the following sentences, using the preposition in brackets and a gerund.

a) The whites took all the land away from the Indians. They didn't ask anybody. (without)

The whites took all the land away from the Indians without asking anybody.

b) Before they took the land, they killed nearly all the buffalo. (before)

c) The Indians needed the buffalo. They couldn't survive without them. (for)

d) First, of course, they ate their meat, but then they also made tents out of their skins. (after)

e) But the whites didn't even eat all the meat; they left the dead buffalo lying on the prairies. (instead of)

f) The whites used the buffalo because they wanted to have fun. (for)

g) But when they killed the buffalo, many whites didn't think of the fact that this would be dangerous for the Indians. (without)

h) Very soon, the Indians realised that the whites would kill them when they killed the buffalo. (by)

i) And that is what really happened. First, the whites nearly destroyed all the buffalo, then they nearly destroyed the Indians. (after)

- Nach vielen Verben, Adjektiven und Nomen mit Präposition musst du ein Gerundium verwenden. Die Beispiele aus den folgenden Listen solltest du daher auswendig lernen.

Verb + Präposition + Gerundium

to agree with	einverstanden sein mit
to believe in	glauben an
to dream of	träumen von
to look forward to	sich freuen auf
to speak of	sprechen von
to succeed in	erfolgreich etwas tun
to think of	denken an
to worry about	sich Sorgen machen um

Adjektiv + Präposition + Gerundium

to be afraid of	Angst haben vor
to be famous for	berühmt sein für
to be fond of	gerne etwas tun
to be good at	etwas gut können
to be interested in	interessiert sein an
to be happy about	glücklich sein über
to be keen on	aus sein auf
to be proud of	stolz sein auf

Nomen + Präposition + Gerundium

chance of	Chance, Aussicht (zu)
danger of	Gefahr (zu)
difficulty in	Schwierigkeit (zu)
idea of	Idee (zu)
opportunity of	Gelegenheit (zu)
possibility of	Möglichkeit (zu)
(no) way of	(keine) Möglichkeit (zu)

- Wie du auf S. 115 f. gesehen hast, ist das Subjekt des Satzes meist auch Handlungsträger des Gerundiums. Die *gerund*-Konstruktion kann aber auch durch ein eigenes **Sinnsubjekt**, d. h. einen eigenen Handlungsträger, ergänzt werden. Dieses Sinnsubjekt erscheint meist im *s*-Genitiv (bei Nomen) bzw. als Possessivpronomen (bei Pronomen).

Beispiele: The Indians relied on the whites' (the whites) being friendly.
At first they didn't mind their (them) shooting some buffalo.

ufgabe 4 John Smart came to the wild west to settle there with his family. He found a great land – but also great problems. Complete the sentences, using the gerund. Sometimes you can (or even have to) use the past form of the gerund.

a) Years later, he at last admitted ______________________ (expect easier life) when ______________________ (first come to the west).

b) The Smarts never spoke ______________________ (Indians be danger) for them, but of course they were happy ______________________ (not be disturbed) by them while ______________________ (build up farm).

c) After ______________________ (come to west), the Smarts had to get used ______________________ (climate be different from that in east).

d) John, who had always been fond ______________________ (can do a lot with wood), was especially proud ______________________ (build whole house alone).

e) However difficult life turned out to be, John never thought ______________________ (his family leave farm again).

f) After the first hard winter, the Smarts were really happy ______________________ (survive), and John knew he would always remember ______________________ (his family nearly die) in those months.

Have you noticed that the sentences don't make too much sense in this order? Find a better one (several solutions are possible).

ufgabe 5* Replace the underlined parts of the following sentences by words and phrases with a gerund.

Not all new settlers <u>managed to</u> live a better life in the west. Many of them said <u>again and again</u> that they <u>liked life in the east better</u>. "<u>Couldn't we</u> go back where we came from?", many women asked their husbands, although they <u>had made the decision</u> to go west together. But the men only answered, "<u>It doesn't help us if</u> we go back. <u>Don't tell me</u> we should leave the west <u>again</u>!" "But we didn't <u>know at all how</u> to keep a farm <u>before we</u> arrived here, and now we see that <u>farming is very difficult for us</u>. <u>I'm sorry, but I always</u> think about how nice life would be elsewhere." "Rubbish! We'll stay here! I think <u>it's good</u> to stay here. And then, <u>you shouldn't</u> worry, but rather go and work, so <u>our chance will be better</u> to have a good harvest this year!"

Not all new settlers succeeded in living a better life in the west.

Aufgabe 6 Complete the dialogues with suitable gerunds. Mind the prepositions.

a)

JENNY: It's no use __________________. The film is sold out.
TOM: But I'm so keen __________________ that film!
JENNY: Well then, how about ________________________ tickets for tomorrow?

b)

BEN: I don't understand how you can enjoy ____________ so much. I can't imagine ____________ here all day!

JILL: Well, I can, though! I've been looking forward ____________ this day at the lake for two weeks.

BEN: But we could do such a lot of things instead ____________ the water for hours! I don't see much chance of your ____________ one single fish!

JILL: Sorry, but it isn't worth while ____________ that with me. I will go on ____________!

c)

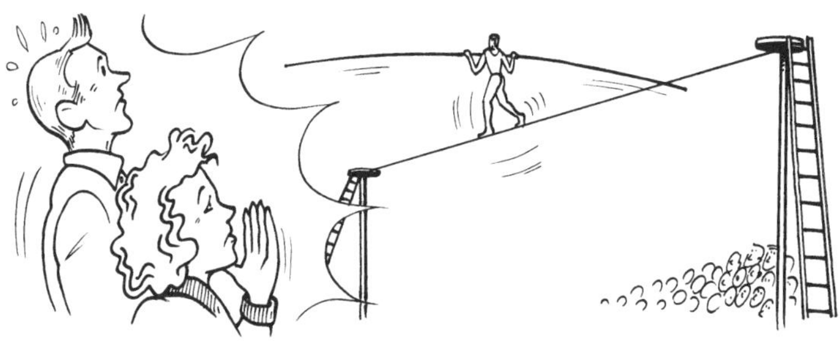

PETER: How does he succeed ____________ on the tightrope without any difficulty?

ANN: Well, of course, he had to practise ____________ so high.

PETER: Yes, but he doesn't even look at the tightrope after ____________ up.

ANN: Perhaps he avoids ____________ down because he is afraid ____________ sick if he does.

PETER: Alright, but at least I wouldn't mind him ____________ a little – he looks so strict!

10.2 Gerundium oder Infinitiv

Wann verwendest du das Gerundium, wann den Infinitiv?

- Viele Verben haben im Deutschen einen Infinitiv nach sich. Dies bedeutet allerdings nicht automatisch, dass diesen Verben auch im Englischen ein Infinitiv folgt – im Gegenteil: Viel häufiger steht das Gerundium.

  Beispiel: Die Indianer vermeiden es, die Weißen anzugreifen.
  The Indians avoided attacking the Whites.

  Du musst also genau unterscheiden, ob im Englischen nach einem Verb das Gerundium oder der Infinitiv steht.
- Nach folgenden Verben kannst du – ohne dass sich die Bedeutung ändert – Gerundium oder Infinitiv verwenden: *to begin, to continue, to hate, to like, to love, to prefer, to start.*

  Beispiel: As soon as they had arrived on the prairies, the whites began shooting/to shoot a lot of buffalo.
- Nach *would hate/like/love/prefer* muss allerdings immer der Infinitiv stehen.

  Beispiel: The Indians said, "We would like to live in peace with you."
- Nach folgenden Verben kann das Gerundium oder der Infinitiv stehen, allerdings **ändert sich dann die Bedeutung des Verbs.**

to forget:	**Vergangenes vergessen** The Indians will never forget seeing their buffalo killed.	**an Zukünftiges nicht denken** The whites should not forget to help the Indians now.
to remember:	**sich an Vergangenes erinnern** Do you remember hearing about the living conditions on the reservations?	**Zukünftiges nicht vergessen** Will American politicians remember to do something for the Indians?
to go on:	**dasselbe weiterhin tun** In spite of the Indians' protest, the whites went on killing buffalo.	**als Nächstes etwas anderes tun** After killing one herd of buffalo, they went on to kill the next.
to stop:	**eine Tätigkeit beenden** We should never stop talking about the Indians.	**innehalten, um Neues zu tun** Take some time; stop to think about the Indians' situation.

fgabe 7 Complete the following story, putting the verbs in brackets into the correct form: infinitive or gerund. Sometimes a preposition will be needed. Keep in mind the rules about infinitives, too.

The first Indian ____________[1] (speak) English

The Pilgrim Fathers established a colony at Plymouth, Massachusetts, in 1619. This was the first English colony ____________[2] (inhabit) for longer than a few months. In Virginia, other colonists continued ____________[3] (live) at Jamestown for some time, but later they did not succeed ____________[4] (create) a permanent settlement.

The Pilgrims were a religious group who wished ____________[5] (separate) from the official Church of England. They were simple people, so they wanted ____________[6] (practise) religion in their own way. Finally the government allowed them ____________[7] (come) to America. They left England in the famous ship "The Mayflower" in June, 1619, ____________[8] (arrive) at Plymouth, Massachusetts, in September of the same year.

The voyage was so difficult that it was impossible for some ____________________ [9] (survive), and in America, too, they had a lot of difficulty ____________________ [10] (survive), as they were not used to ____________________ [11] (live) this sort of life. Winter soon set in, and their food gave out. Many became sick and died.

One day in early spring, an Indian appeared and said in English, "Welcome!". The Pilgrims were very much surprised ____________________ [12] (hear) that. The Indian knew a few more words of English and was able ____________________ [13] (explain) that he had a friend who spoke English well. In a few days this friend, called Squanto, arrived. Some fifteen years earlier, he and four other Indians had been picked up by an English ship and taken, as prisoners, to England, where he had had ____________________ [14] (stay) for nine years. Then John Smith brought him back to America in 1614, because he had promised ____________________ [15] (return) Squanto to his people. Another captain, Thomas Hunt, recaptured Squanto and fifteen other Indians and carried them to Spain. Some Spanish priests helped him ____________________ [16] (finally make) his way back to England. In 1619, he was again brought back to America.

Squanto was of great help to the Pilgrims. When he met them, he seemed happy ____________________ [17] (be) among them. He settled down immediately with them and stayed with them for the rest of his life.

He taught the Pilgrims where and how ____________________ [18] (fish). He liked ____________________ [19] (act) as their guide through the forests. He was fond ____________________ [20] (be) their interpreter with the different Indian tribes. Most important of all, he taught the Pilgrims how ____________________ [21] (plant) corn. He showed them how, in ____________________ [22] (plant) this corn, they must put two small fish in each hill of corn in order ____________________ [23] (make) the soil rich.

It is possible that without Squanto ____________________ [24] (help), the colony at Plymouth would have failed. He made them ____________________ [25] (get) through their first few years. They needed ____________________ [26] (help), and he was keen ____________________ [27] (give) his help. After his death, the Pilgrims honored him ____________________ [28] (bury) him among their own people.

Aufgabe 8 The gerund & infinitive alphabet. Choose the right forms of the verb *to tell* that go with the 25 beginnings of sentences.

They **a**voided …	telling	their parents about it.
They were **b**usy …	______	
They **c**ouldn't …	______	
They didn't **d**are …	______	
They **e**xpected me …	______	
They **f**orgot …	______	
They **g**ave up …	______	
They were **h**appy …	______	
They couldn't **i**magine …	______	
They were **j**ustified …	______	
They were **k**een on …	______	
They **l**et me …	______	
They **m**ade me …	______	
It was **n**o good …	______	
I **o**rdered them …	______	
They **p**referred …	______	
I wasn't **q**ualified …	______	
They **r**emembered …	______	
They **s**topped …	______	
They were **t**old …	______	
It was **u**nusual for them …	______	
They were **v**icious enough …	______	
They laughed **w**hen …	______	
They were too **y**oung …	______	
They were **z**ealous …	______	

Can you imagine what their parents got to know in the end, or what they didn't get to know?

Aufgabe 9 Translate, using gerunds and infinitives wherever possible.

Bevor er in Amerika landete, war Kolumbus monatelang auf See. Er und seine Männer hatten Schwierigkeiten zu überleben und in seinem Tagebuch beklagte er sich immer wieder, dass sie schlechtes Wasser trinken mussten. Aber der spanische König hatte ihnen versprochen, sie reich zu machen, und so hörten sie nicht auf, auf bessere Zeiten zu hoffen; schließlich erwartete der König von ihnen, ihre Reise zu Ende zu führen. Die Seeleute verließen sich darauf, dass die Hoffnungen ihres Kapitäns begründet (= founded) waren. Später erinnerte sich Kolumbus daran, wie er endlich Land gesehen hatte. Es fiel ihm schwer zu glauben, dass es ihm wirklich gelungen war, seinen Plan in die Tat umzusetzen.

11 Partizip

Im Englischen gibt es zwei Grundformen des Partizips: das **Partizip Präsens** und das **Partizip Perfekt**. Diese beiden Partizipien unterscheiden sich nicht zeitlich voneinander, sondern vielmehr darin, dass das Partizip Präsens **aktivische Bedeutung** und das Partizip Perfekt **passivische Bedeutung** hat.

Beispiele: This lady selling clothes is a friend of ours. *(present participle)*
She likes the job given to her very much. *(past participle)*

Wann verwendest du die beiden Partizipien?

- Einige Partizipien, sowohl Präsens- als auch Perfektformen, kannst du wie Adjektive, also **vor einem Nomen** verwenden.

  Beispiel: My grandfather is known as the singing cook.

- Andere Partizipien sind zu **echten Adjektiven oder Bestandteilen von Adjektiven** geworden. Diese kannst du dann auch steigern.

  Beispiel: Collecting stamps is the most boring activity I know.

- Die Partizipien können auch **nach einem Nomen** stehen. Mit einer solchen Partizipial-Konstruktion kannst du notwendige Relativsätze, bei denen das Relativpronomen Subjekt des Satzes ist, wie folgt auflösen:

  Partizip Präsens
  Zur Auflösung eines Relativsatzes im Aktiv verwendest du das Partizip Präsens. Das Relativpronomen und das Hilfsverb – sofern eines vorhanden ist – fallen dabei weg.

  Beispiel: The man who lives next door to us is a mechanic.
  The man living next door to us is a mechanic.

  Partizip Perfekt
  Zur Auflösung eines Relativsatzes im Passiv verwendest du das Partizip Perfekt. Hier musst du das Relativpronomen und die Form von *to be* weglassen.

  Beispiel: He works at a garage which is owned by his uncle.
  He works at a garage owned by his uncle.

Wie bildest du die Partizipien?

- Das **Partizip Präsens** ist eine weitere *ing*-Form des Verbs (siehe S. 47).
- Das **Partizip Perfekt** wird gebildet aus dem Infinitiv + *-ed* bzw. ist die 3. Form der unregelmäßigen Verben.

Aufgabe 1 Little Jenny's jobs (I)

Little Jenny is four. She has a lot of ideas about her future, so she has painted pictures of what she might want to be. She explains these jobs to her father, and he tells her what they are called. Write down what they say, using present participles.

a) 

JENNY: *This is a woman watering …* ______________________________.

FATHER: *I see. This is a* ______________________________.

b) 

JENNY: ______________________________

FATHER: ______________________________

c) 

JENNY: ______________________________

FATHER: ______________________________

d) 

JENNY: ______________________________

FATHER: ______________________________

e) 

JENNY: ______________________________
____

FATHER: ______________________________
____

f) 

JENNY: ______________________________
____

FATHER: ______________________________
____

Aufgabe 2 Little Jenny's jobs (II)

A few days later, Jenny is proud to remember all those jobs. So she paints new pictures and explains them to her mother. Write down what she says, using past participles.

a) 

JENNY: These are the flowers watered by ______________________________.

b) 

JENNY: ______________________________
____

c)

JENNY: ______________________

____

d)

JENNY: ______________________

____

e)

JENNY: ______________________

____

f)

JENNY: ______________________

____

- Partizipien kannst du auch zur **Verkürzung adverbialer Nebensätze** verwenden.

Beispiele: Truckers are happiest when they drive around the country.
Truckers are happiest driving around the country.
(zeitlicher Bezug)

They always do their job and drive for hours without interruption.
They always do their job driving for hours without interruption.
(Art und Weise)

But they go on, because they want to be independent.
But they go on, wanting to be independent.
(Grund)

Aufgabe 3 Rewrite the following text, using participles whenever possible. In the first few sentences, the passages which you can replace are underlined.

<u>As she wants</u> to buy herself a motor-bike, Amy does everything this year to find a good holiday job. Still, she doesn't want to take the one <u>her uncle offered her</u> in his grocer's shop: <u>when she works</u> eight hours a day, she wants to earn more than £ 100 a week! <u>While she is reading</u> the newspaper one morning, she suddenly sees an advert which says: "Are you one of those youngsters who are looking for a job? You don't like any of the jobs that are advertised for in the papers? And you don't like jobs which only get you little money? Then come and see us immediately! The workers at our petrol station are really happy because they are paid extremely well!"
Amy went there, and she got a job. This is how she made a lot of money: she washed cars, checked the oil and cleaned windscreens. And after the holidays, she was very proud, so she said to her uncle: "I will never work for somebody who pays his workers as badly as you do!"

Aufgabe 4 Translate. Use participles whenever possible.

Wenn sie von einem tollen Beruf träumen, denken viele Jugendliche daran, Stewardess oder Steward zu werden. Sie haben gehört, dass man viel Spaß hat, wenn man von einem Land ins andere fliegt. Aber sie vergessen, dass es auch harte Arbeit ist, wenn man stundenlang den Passagieren Essen und Getränke servieren muss. Außerdem verdienen nur die Stewards und Stewardessen viel, die bei großen Fluggesellschaften angestellt sind. Weil sie enttäuscht von ihrer Arbeit sind, suchen sich viele Stewards und Stewardessen nach ein paar Jahren eine andere Stelle, die ihnen mehr bietet. Schließlich muss man wissen, dass die Fluggesellschaften nur gut ausgebildete junge Frauen und Männer nehmen, die Fremdsprachen sprechen.

Aufgabe 5 The Story of Daniel Boone

First read the text carefully. Then answer the questions, using participles in your answers.

People who lead the way are called pioneers. The first colonists who came to the east were pioneers. They settled along the Atlantic Coast in what was then a forest area, and they changed it into a land of towns and farms. To the west they saw the Appalachian Mountains rising. Across the mountains lay another forest, which was then called the American Frontier.

The mountains that separated this forest from the thirteen American colonies were steep and difficult to cross. Indians who lived in the area west of the mountains had said that they would always keep the white men out. But a few brave hunters fought the Indians as they crossed the mountains. One of the pioneers who led the way was Daniel Boone.

It was during the French and Indian War, in 1762, that Boone (who always worked very hard) met a person who was to change his whole life – John Findlay, a scout and Indian fighter, who had been to the west of the mountains, and he had returned with stories of the beautiful land that the Indians called Kentucky. As he talked a lot about it to Boone, he filled Daniel's head with the idea of moving to Kentucky.

Many years went by before Boone was able to lead his own family and other families to Kentucky; he organized a wagon trail to the land of his dreams. In 1775, Daniel Boone, his wife, two sons and a daughter, and some of his friends started a settlement which they called Boonesborough, and it grew fast. Largely through the efforts of Daniel Boone, which he had planned for a long time, and those of a few other brave pioneers like him, the way to the west was now open, an adventure which began the growth of the United States in this direction.

a) Who are pioneers?

People leading the way are called pioneers. / We call people leading the way pioneers.

b) Can we call the first American colonists pioneers?

____

c) What did they do?

____

d) What was across the Appalachian Mountains?

____

e) Why did they stay at the coast for a long time?

f) Were the Indians friendly?

g) Did this keep the whites back?

h) Who was Daniel Boone?

i) Describe John Findlay.

j) What made Daniel Boone want to move to Kentucky?

k) Did the Boones go to Kentucky alone?

l) What happened in 1775?

m) What do you know about Boonesborough?

n) What were Boone's efforts like, and why were they so important for the future of the United States?

Auf Seite 112 hast du gesehen, dass die Verben *to let* und *to make* (‚lassen') im Englischen und im Deutschen mit einem Infinitiv verbunden werden. Auch die Partizipialkonstruktion *to have sth. done (have* + Objekt + Partizip Perfekt) wird im Deutschen mit ‚lassen' wiedergegeben.

Beispiel: I don't want to have my car repaired by an apprentice.

Beachte den Bedeutungsunterschied:

- My parents won't let me leave school before I get some qualifications.
  ‚zulassen', ‚erlauben' mit Infinitiv ohne *to*
- They will make me attend school until I get some qualifications.
  ‚veranlassen' mit Infinitiv ohne to
- But I don't want to be made to stay there as long as that.
  ‚veranlasst werden' mit Infinitiv mit *to* (Passiv)
- I want to start working at the garage where my father always has his car repaired.
  ‚veranlassen, dass etwas getan wird' *have* + Objekt + Partizip Perfekt

ufgabe 6 Describe the scenes, using the correct word for 'lassen' and suitable verbs.

a)

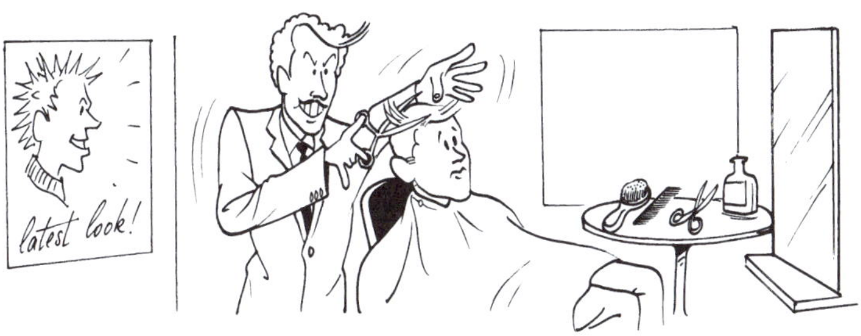

The man has ______________________________

b)

The boss ______________________________

c)

The boss ______________________________

d)

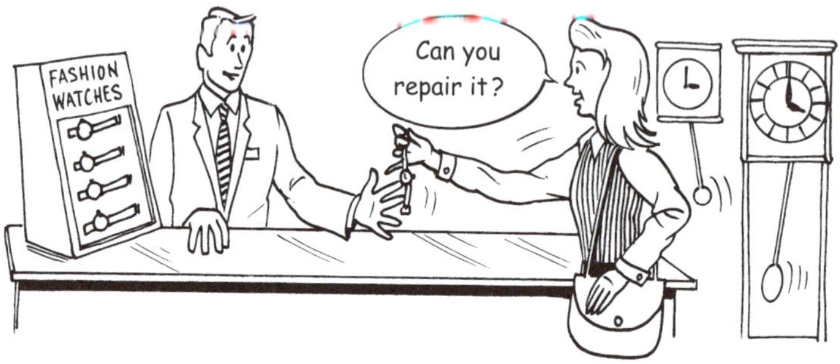

The lady ______________________________

e)

The workers ______________________________

f)

The gardener doesn't ______________________________

… rund um den Satz

12 Relativsätze

Relativsätze sind Nebensätze, die zusätzliche Informationen über die Sache oder die Person, die direkt davor genannt ist, geben. Relativsätze werden meist von Relativpronomen (*who, that, whose, which*) eingeleitet.

- **Notwendige Relativsätze** (*defining relative clauses*) geben Informationen, die **unerlässlich für den Sinn** des Satzes sind. Anders als deutsche Relativsätze stehen sie nicht zwischen Kommas.

  Beispiel: Elizabeth I was the English queen who started the growth of the British Empire.

- **Nicht-notwendige Relativsätze** (*non-defining relative clauses*) geben Informationen, ohne die der Satz – auch im Zusammenhang – noch immer sinnvoll ist. Sie stehen zwischen Kommas.

  Beispiel: Elizabeth I, who was born in 1533, started the growth of the British Empire.

12.1 Relativpronomen

Wann verwendest du *who, whom, which, that* und *whose?*

- ***who*** verwendest du nur für **Personen**. Es kann im Relativsatz sowohl **Subjekt** als auch **Objekt** sein. Für Personen kannst du als **Objekt auch *whom*** verwenden.

  Beispiele: The queen who gave orders to Sir Francis Drake to sail round the world was Elizabeth I. (*who* = Subjekt)
  Sir Francis Drake, who/whom Elizabeth had given orders to head west, sailed round the world. (*who /whom = Objekt*)

- ***which*** verwendest du nur für **Dinge**. Auch *which* kannst du als **Subjekt** und als **Objekt** im Relativsatz benutzen.

  Beispiele: In 1587, Drake defeated the Armada, which was led by King Philip II.
  (which = Subjekt)
  Drake was very sad about the two ships which he lost on a voyage in 1577.
  (which = Objekt)

- ***that*** kannst du für **Personen** und **Dinge** in **notwendigen Relativsätzen** verwenden. Hier ist ebenfalls der Gebrauch als Subjekt und als Objekt möglich.

  Beispiele: The man that was knighted in 1580 was F. Drake. *(that = Subjekt)*
  He was unhappy about the ships that he lost. *(that = Objekt)*

- Der **Relativbegleiter *whose*** (deutsch: ‚deren', ‚dessen') kann in Verbindung mit einem Nomen für **Personen** oder **Sachen** stehen.

  Beispiele: Queen Victoria, whose husband was from Germany, reigned for over 60 years.
  The ship whose officer was Francis Drake was called 'Victory'.

Aufgabe 1 Match each picture from the left column with one from the right column and make sentences, starting with what you see on the left. Use *who*, *whom* or *which* as relative pronouns.

a)

(1)

b)

(2)

c) 

(3) 

d) 

(4) 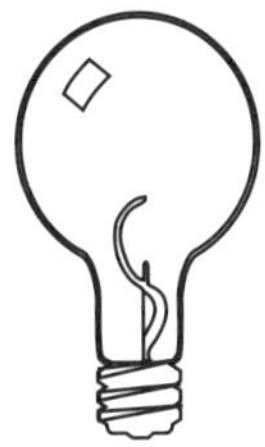

e) 

(5) 

f) 

(6) 

a) Model T is the car ______________________________

b) Alexander Bell ______________________________

c) ______________________________

d) Thomas Alva Edison ______________________________

e) ______________________________ Clara Barton.

f) ______________________________ (active and passive)

Aufgabe 2 The following sentences tell you something about a few famous Britons and Americans. Can you find out their names? Which of the relative pronouns can be replaced with *that*?

a) 

This man, whose son was kidnapped in 1932, was the first man who flew from the USA to Europe alone.

Name: ______________________

b) 

As she helped the men who were wounded in the Crimean War, this woman, who was born in 1820, became known as "the lady with the lamp".

Name: ______________________

c) 

He is the man whose most famous piece of writing was the Declaration of Independence.

Name: ______________________

d) 

This woman, whose son is Prince Charles, became Queen of England in 1952.

Name: ______________________

e) 

Vicksburg is the town which was captured by this Unionist general in the American Civil War.
Name: ____________________

f) 

The discovery which made this man rich was that rubber is a material whose qualities make it ideal for the production of tyres.
Name: ____________________

g) 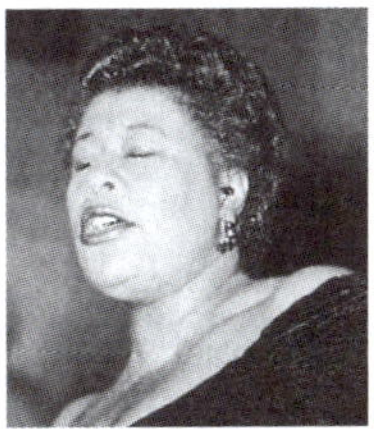

The name which was given to this woman was "First Lady of Jazz".
Name: ____________________

h) 

Trafalgar is the battle which this man won, but which he was also killed in.
Name: ____________________

Aufgabe 3 Put in suitable relative pronouns.

When English settlers in America founded Jamestown Colony in 1607, all of the area ______________ [1] was around it was occupied by Indian tribes. The powerful chief ____________________ [2] headed these tribes was known as Powhatan. He and his people were generally friendly towards the pioneers, __________________ [3] first few years were difficult indeed.

Powhatan had a very soft heart for his "dearest daughter", Pocahontas, ______________ [4] was about 13 years old at the time the English arrived. Many

legends have been passed down to us about Pocahontas, for example that of Captain John Smith, __________[5] the Indians captured and wanted to kill, and __________[6] life Pocahontas saved by throwing herself over his body.
When relations between the English and the Indians deteriorated, the English developed a plan with __________[7] to recover the goods and prisoners __________[8] the Indians had taken from them. They persuaded Pocahontas to board a British ship __________[9] lay at anchor in the Potomac river and sailed to Jamestown with her. Thus, the girl __________[10] was so loved by her father was an English hostage. But at Jamestown she met John Rolfe, __________[11] is described as an "honest gentleman and of good behaviour". The two fell in love, and were married. Thus, Powhatan kept peace with the English colonists until his death in 1618.

12.2 *contact clauses*

Was sind *contact clauses*?

Ist das **Relativpronomen Objekt eines notwendigen Relativsatzes**, kannst du es auch weglassen. Relativsätze ohne Relativpronomen nennt man *contact clauses*. Sie beginnen stets mit einem eigenen Subjekt.

Beispiele:	Albert was the man	whom	Victoria really loved.
	Albert was the man	–	Victoria really loved.
		object	*subject*

Aufgabe 4 Put in suitable relative pronouns and state whether the pronoun can be left out (contact clauses). Insert commas where necessary.

We know a lot __________[1] is interesting about the Celts, __________[2] were the early inhabitants of England before the Germanic tribes __________[3] had

set out from what is now Northern Germany began to inhabit the island ______________[4] has always been of strategic interest for all peoples.
The Celts ______________[5] origins are probably in regions ______________[6] now lie in central France came to England as early as the seventh century before Christ. They were a people ______________[7] influence at its peak (around 300 B. C.) extended through the whole of Europe. A great part of the works of art ______________[8] the Celts produced can still be seen today. There are all kinds of jewellery on ______________[9] we find beautiful ornamentation and symmetrical patterns.
The language ______________[10] the Celts spoke has not disappeared either. Welsh, Scottish and Irish are living languages ______________[11] origin is the old Celtic language. There are some characteristics of Celtic ______________[12] can still be found in these languages.
Religion is one part of Celtic life ______________[13] we do not know everything about. We can only guess that the Celts had some gods ______________[14] other religions knew, too. It is interesting that the importance of women ______________[15] had a very high social position in Celtic life was reflected in the fact that many of the gods of ______________[16] we know are female.

12.3 Präpositionen in Relativsätzen

An welcher Stelle stehen in den Relativsätzen die Präpositionen?

- Im Unterschied zu den deutschen Relativsätzen, in denen die Präpositionen immer vor dem Relativpronomen stehen, stehen die **Präpositionen** im Englischen **meist hinter dem Verb des Relativsatzes**.

  Beispiel: The man (who) Queen Victoria was married to was Prince Albert.

  Du kennst diese Endstellung der Präposition schon von Fragen mit einem Fragewort.

  Beispiele: Where are you from? (Von wo/woher …)
  Who do you want to talk to? (Mit wem …)

- Im **formellen Englisch** kannst du die Präpositionen auch **vor die Relativpronomen *whom*** und ***which*** stellen.

  Beispiel: The man to whom she was married was Prince Albert.

- Steht das Relativpronomen ***that*** in einem Relativsatz, musst du die Präposition **hinter das Verb** stellen.

  Beispiel: The man that she was married to …

Aufgabe 5 Look at what Uncle Sam says about the USA, and use his sentences to make constructions with a relative clause. Start your sentences with the underlined words. Mind the prepositions!

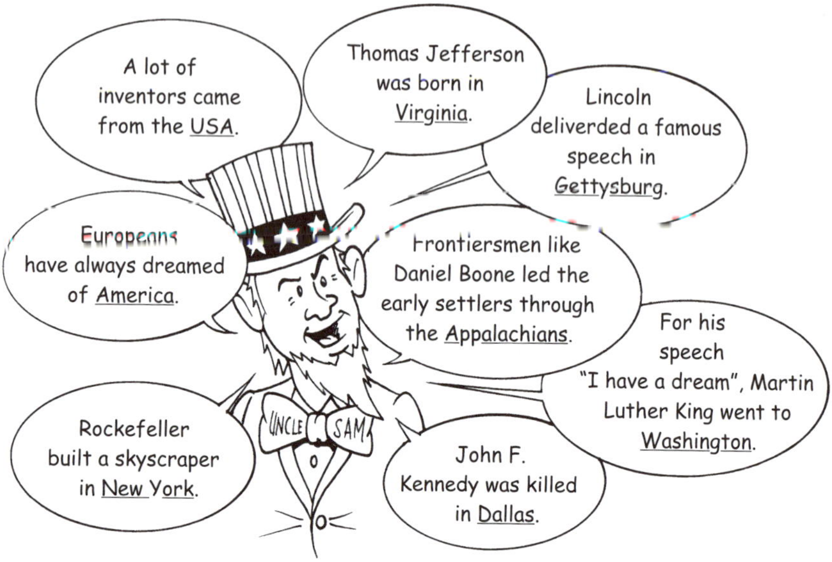

a) New York is the city *Rockefeller built a skyscraper in. / … in which Rockefeller built a skyscraper.*

b) America is ______

c) ______

d) ______

e) ______

f) ______

g) ______

h) ______

ufgabe 6 Look again at exercise 2. Use the information which you get there to answer the following questions. Don't forget to use a relative clause with a preposition in each of your answers. Indicate whether you can leave out the relative pronoun.

a) What adventure did Charles Lindbergh succeed in?
The adventure Lindbergh succeeded in was to fly from the USA to Europe alone.
(in which Lindbergh succeeded)

b) By what name was Florence Nightingale called?

c) What piece of writing did Thomas Jefferson become famous for?

d) Look at the woman in the fourth picture. Who is she?

e) Vicksburg was captured by a man. Who was he?

f) What product is rubber ideal for?

g) What name was Ella Fitzgerald known by?

h) Horatio Nelson was killed in a battle. Where did it take place?

ufgabe 7 Translate. Leave out the relative pronoun if possible.

Horatio Nelson, dessen Eltern ihn in Norfolk zur Schule schickten, ging 1770, mit 12 Jahren, zur Marine. Der Bruder seiner Mutter, der selbst (Marine-)Kapitän war, half ihm. Das einzige Problem, das er in seinem ganzen Leben nicht lösen konnte, war seine Seekrankheit, wegen der (= für die) er von vielen belächelt wurde: Nelson, der Großbritanniens größter Marineoffizier werden sollte, kämpfte ständig gegen die Übelkeit! Die Schlacht, mit der Nelson schließlich berühmt wurde, fand 1805 statt. Das Schiff, mit dem er in die Schlacht von Trafalgar segelte, hieß „Victory". Er besiegte Frankreich und Spanien, die 33 Schiffe geschickt hatten. England war vor Napoleon gerettet, der nun auf dem europäischen Festland bleiben musste.

Wie bildest du eine Konstruktion mit einem Relativsatz?

Um aus zwei Sätzen einen Satz mit Relativkonstruktion zu machen, musst du zunächst das gemeinsame Element in beiden Sätzen suchen. In dem Satz, der Relativsatz wird, musst du dann dieses gemeinsame Element durch das passende Relativpronomen ersetzen.

Beispiel: Prince Philip is from Germany. He is Queen Elizabeth II's husband.
(beiden Sätzen gemeinsam: Prince Philip)
Prince Philip, who is Queen Elizabeth II's husband, is from Germany.

Aufgabe 8 Growth of the USA: The Louisiana[1] Purchase

Put the sentences together, using one of them as a relative clause. Decide whether you must use commas or not. Indicate whether you can leave out the relative pronoun.

a) After the American Revolution, the country grew, and its western frontier was the Mississippi. Before, it had been a small territory along the Atlantic coast.

b) The second great step was the Louisiana Purchase. With this purchase, the size of the country was suddenly increased by one third.

c) The exact western limits of the new territory were not known; the treaty was not clear on its exact western limits.

d) The important fact was that no strong foreign power held territory to the west of the young United States. The young United States was free to grow in the direction of the Pacific.

1 Louisiana: at that time, Louisiana extended from the Canadian border to the Gulf of Mexico

e) The Louisiana territory was bought in 1803. There was little interest in this territory.

f) The land was unknown to most Americans. It seemed very far away to most Americans.

g) But the Mississippi was of importance to many of the settlers of Kentucky and Tennessee. These settlers had no other way of selling their farm products but to ship them down the Mississippi to New Orleans.

h) But many times the port of New Orleans was closed to American shipping by Spanish officials there. They were often changed by the government in Spain, others suddenly closed the port without explanation.

i) President Jefferson was also worried about Napoleon Bonaparte. The Spanish would soon hand over the territory to Napoleon Bonaparte.

j) A foreign power controlled the Mississippi and New Orleans. Any foreign power was a danger to the United States.

k) So Jefferson advised Robert Livingston to make an offer to buy the city of New Orleans. Robert Livingston was the American ambassador to France.

l) Napoleon considered the offer. Napoleon's wars in Europe were very costly.

m) He found one thing out about the territory of Louisiana: he couldn't really use it, and he could make a lot of money with it.

n) So he offered the Americans the purchase of the whole of Louisiana, but not all Americans favored the purchase.

o) The price was $ 15 million. The French and the Americans finally agreed upon it.

p) The territory included nearly a million square miles. Jefferson purchased the territory.

q) The land cost the Americans less than four cents an acre. In all, thirteen states were formed from this land.

a) After the American Revolution, the country, which had been a small territory along the Atlantic coast before, grew, and its western frontier was the Mississippi.

b) ______________________________

____

c) ______________________________

____

d) ______________________________

____

e) ______________________________

____

f) ______________________________

____

g) ______________________________

____

h) ______________________________

____

i) ______________________________

____

j) ______________________________

____

k) ______________________________

____

l) ______________________________

____

m) ______________________________

____

n) ______________________________

____

o) ______________________________

____

p) ______________________________

____

q) ______________________________

____

Tipps zum sinngemäßen Übertragen von Texten *(mediation)*

In der Schule werden die Unterschiede zwischen der englischen und der deutschen Sprache oft an Hand von Übersetzungen verdeutlicht. Wenn du jedoch selbst mit Menschen sprichst, die nur Englisch, aber kein Deutsch können, oder wenn du dolmetschen musst, wird es für dich weniger darum gehen, wortgenau zu übersetzen; viel wichtiger ist es dann, **die entscheidenden Gedanken des Gesagten oder Geschriebenen sinngemäß in der anderen Sprache wiederzugeben**. Auch das – in der Fachsprache *mediation* genannt – muss geübt werden, und du solltest unbedingt ein paar Dinge beachten:

- Du bist bei der *mediation* wesentlich **freier als beim Übersetzen**, was die sprachliche Gestaltung anbelangt; trotzdem solltest du dich **nicht zu weit vom Original entfernen**, weil du sonst Gefahr läufst, Wichtiges zu vergessen.
- Es kann sinnvoll sein, **aus zwei Sätzen einen** zu machen.
- Umgekehrt darfst du auch **einen Satz oder Satzteil ausführlicher übertragen**, wenn du den Eindruck hast, er wäre sonst unverständlich.
- Du darfst auch die **Reihenfolge des Gesagten oder Geschriebenen ändern**, wenn es dir hilft, einen logischen Text zu erstellen.
- Du musst nicht für jedes Wort in der einen Sprache das genaue Gegenstück in der anderen finden; andererseits genügt es nicht, immer nur zu umschreiben.
- **Lies am Ende deinen Text nochmals gründlich** durch und vergewissere dich, dass du keine entscheidenden Punkte vergessen hast und dass der Gedankengang immer noch logisch und verständlich ist.

ufgabe 9* Read the story of the Louisiana Purchase again (exercise 8, p. 148/149) and retell it in German. Be careful: this is not a translation exercise!

13 Indirekte Rede

Die indirekte Rede *(reported speech)* ist eine Form der **Redeerwähnung:** Innerhalb einer Äußerung wird auf eine andere Äußerung eingegangen.

Wann verwendest du die indirekte Rede?

Du gebrauchst die **indirekte Rede** (*reported speech*), **um zu berichten, was ein anderer – oder du selbst – gesagt hat, sagt oder sagen wird**. Die indirekte Rede verwendest du also anstelle der wörtlichen Rede (*direct speech*), die in Anführungszeichen steht.

Beispiel: I always say, "Children must learn a lot!" *(direct speech)*
I always say that children must learn a lot. *(reported speech)*

Wie bildest du die indirekte Rede?

Du bildest die **indirekte Rede** aus einem **Einleitungssatz mit Einleitungsverben** wie *say*, *ask*, *report* und einem ***that*-Satz**. Im Englischen musst du als Erstes auf die Zeit achten, in der der Einleitungssatz steht.

- Steht der **Einleitungssatz im *present tense*, *present perfect*** oder im ***will-future***, unterscheidet sich der Satz in der indirekten Rede von dem in der wörtlichen Rede nur in Hinsicht auf die **Pronomen** und **Begleiter**.

  Beispiele: He says, "I want to go dancing." *(direct speech)*
  (Einleitungssatz im *present tense*)
  He says that he wants to go dancing. *(reported speech)*
  He has always said, "I liked this film." *(direct speech)*
  (Einleitungssatz im *present perfect*)
  He has always said that he liked that film. *(reported speech)*
  He will say, "You can come to my party." *(direct speech)*
  (Einleitungssatz im will-future)
  He will say that I can come to his party. *(reported speech)*

Aufgabe 1 Write down what Cindy says (clockwise). Use reported speech.

a) Cindy says that she *is sure she'll get a good job as an apprentice.*

b) ______________________________

c) ______________________________

d) ______________________________

e) ______________________________

f) ______________________________

g) ______________________________

- Steht der **Einleitungssatz im *past tense, past perfect*** oder ***conditional***, müssen bei der Übertragung in die indirekte Rede neben den Pronomen bzw. Begleitern auch die **Zeiten** verändert werden:

present	→	*past*
alle Vergangenheitszeiten	→	*past perfect* (vgl. S. 59 und S. 61)
future	→	*conditional* (vgl. S. 77 und S. 79)

Beispiele:

Ken said to me: "You are lovely." *(simple present)*
Ken told me that I was lovely. *(simple past)*

He added: "I'm going to the cinema." *(present progressive)*
He added that he was going to the cinema. *(past progressive)*

I said: "I didn't want to go dancing." *(simple past)*
I said that I hadn't wanted to go dancing. *(past perfect)*

He answered: "I was kidding." *(past progressive)*
He answered he had been kidding. *(past perfect progressive)*

He had already warned me: "We have already seen this film." *(present perfect simple)*
He had already warned me that we had already seen that film. *(past perfect simple)*

I said: "He has been talking to me." *(present perfect progressive)*
I said that he had been talking to me. *(past perfect progressive)*

I would have liked to say: "Tom had asked me earlier." *(past perfect simple)*
I would have liked to tell him that Tom had asked me earlier. *(past perfect simple)*

But I thought: "He had been asking other girls for days." *(past perfect progressive)*
I thought he had been asking other girls for days. *(past perfect progressive)*

Then I said: "I will go with you." *(will-future)*
Then I said I would go with him. *(conditional)*

He replied: "You'll soon have seen the best of all films." *(future perfect)*
He promised that I would soon have seen the best of all films. *(conditional perfect)*

In der indirekten Rede mit Einleitungssatz in der Vergangenheit stehen also nur *past tense, past perfect* sowie *conditional* und *conditional perfect. Past perfect, conditional* und *conditional perfect* aus der wörtlichen Rede bleiben erhalten.

Aufgabe 2 This morning I met Cindy – do you remember her from exercise 1? She told me all about her plans and dreams. What did she say?

a) She said that she was sure she would get a good job as an apprentice.

b) ______

c) ______

d) ______

e) ______

f) ______

g) ______

Aufgabe 3 Here is an excerpt from Adrian Mole's secret diary, a book written by Sue Townsend. In it, Adrian wrote about Pandora, the girl he loved. Write down what he wrote, using reported speech.

Friday July 17th

FULL MOON

My precious love leaves these shores tomorrow. I'm going to the airport to see her off. I hope her plane won't suffer from metal fatigue. I have just checked the world map to see where Tunisia is, and I am most relieved to see that Pandora won't have to fly through the Bermuda triangle.
If anything happened to my love I would never smile again.
I have bought her a book to read during the flight. It is called *Crash!*, by a bloke called William Goldenstein, III. It is very good on what to do if the worst happens.

Saturday July 18th

Pandora read the *Crash!* book in the coach on the way to the airport. When her flight was called she had slight hysterics and her father had to carry her up the steps. I waved to the plane until it had retreated into a large cloud, then I sadly got on a coach and came back home. How I will get through the next fortnight I don't know. Goodnight, my Tunisian beauty.
(From: Sue Townsend, The Secret Diary of Adrian Mole Aged 13 ¾, London, Methuen, p. 101/102)

On Friday, Adrian wrote that his precious love left the town the next day.

Die folgenden Regeln musst du bei allen Sätzen in der indirekten Rede beachten:

- ***that*** kannst du auch **weglassen**.

  Beispiel: They never tell me (that) I must stay at home.

- Bei **Fragen** in der indirekten Rede (indirekte Fragen) steht **keine Form von *to do***. Die Wortstellung entspricht der im Aussagesatz (SVO).

  Beispiel: "Where did you come from?"
  We always wonder where you came from.

- Bei **Fragen mit einem Fragewort** bleibt dieses in der indirekten Frage erhalten. Bei **Entscheidungsfragen** (Antwort ja oder nein) musst du ***if*** oder ***whether*** verwenden.

  Beispiele: Sometimes my parents ask me, "Whom are you going to meet?"
  Sometimes my parents ask me whom I am going to meet.
  I will ask them: "Are you ready?"
  I will ask them if/whether they are ready.

- Sind Subjekt des Einleitungssatzes und des Fragesatzes gleich, steht nach dem Fragewort der Infinitiv.

  Beispiel: She never wonders, "What will I do?"
  She never wonders what to do.

- Auch **Befehle und Aufforderungen** werden in der indirekten Rede **mit** dem **Infinitiv** wiedergegeben.

  Beispiel: My father always says: "Go to bed early!"
  My father always tells me to go to bed early.

- Folgende Verben können eine indirekte Rede einleiten. Lerne sie auswendig!
  to add, to advise, to answer, to ask (auch im Sinne von ‚bitten'), *to cry, to hear, to invite, to want to know, to mention, to offer, to point out, to remark, to reply, to say, to scream, to shout, to suggest, to tell s.b., to think, to wonder*, u. v. a.

  Auch nach Verben der Sinneswahrnehmung (*to see, to feel* usw.) folgt ein *that*-Satz den Regeln der indirekten Rede.

  Beispiel: I saw that she was watching TV.

Aufgabe 4 Pocket money

Here is a dialogue between Mathew, 13, and his mother, Mrs Brown – one of those typical dialogues which happen again and again in many families. Write down what Mrs Brown told her husband about their conversation in the evening. Use different reporting verbs.

MATHEW:	Mum, I want more pocket money.
MRS BROWN:	What did you say?
MATHEW:	I'd like to have more pocket money.
MRS BROWN:	Well, first tell me why you want more.
MATHEW:	I haven't got enough to buy myself all the things I want.
MRS BROWN:	What do you want to buy?
MATHEW:	I don't know, CDs, books, …
MRS BROWN:	But I give you fifteen pounds every month, that must be enough.
MATHEW:	But all my classmates get much more!
MRS BROWN:	Who gets how much?
MATHEW:	I think Andy got thirty pounds last month.
MRS BROWN:	That's what you think! Ask him if you don't really know!
MATHEW:	But, please, Mum, give me a little more!
MRS BROWN:	Okay, how much shall I give you? I'll give you twenty pounds next month. Is that all right?
MATHEW:	Oh, that's great, thank you, Mum!

Mathew told me that he wanted more pocket money.

Die folgenden Regeln gelten nur bei indirekter Rede mit **Einleitungssatz in der Vergangenheit**.

- Du musst bei einem Einleitungssatz in der Vergangenheit auch die **modalen Hilfsverben** wie folgt verändern:

can, could	→	could
may, might	→	might
shall, should	→	should
will, would	→	would

Beispiel: Kevin asked his dad: "May I go to the disco?"
Kevin asked his dad if he might go to the disco.

- Bei *must, mustn't* und *needn't* musst du und bei *can* kannst du die **Ersatzformen** verwenden.

Beispiele: So Kevin told his friends: "I can come to the disco, but I must be at home by twelve; you needn't collect me."
So Kevin told his friends that he could/was allowed to come to the disco, but that he had to be at home by twelve; they didn't have to collect him.

- Auch **Zeit- und Ortsangaben** musst du verändern:

today	→	that day
tonight	→	that evening
yesterday	→	the day before
tomorrow	→	the next/following day
this (week)	→	that (week)
(2 years) ago	→	(2 years) before
next (month)	→	the following (month)
last (time)	→	(the time) before
here	→	there

Beispiel: Peggy rang up her boyfriend and said to him: "I can't come to your place today."
Peggy rang up her boyfriend and told him that she couldn't come to his place that day.

Aufgabe 5 Last Tuesday, Wendy wanted to go to a pop concert, but her father wasn't really happy about it. A few days later, she wrote a letter to a friend and complained to her about the discussion with her father. Write this passage for her. Use different reporting verbs.

FATHER: What are you going to do tonight?

WENDY: Haven't I told you about that pop concert? I'm sure it will be great!

FATHER: Pop concert? I don't want you to go to pop concerts when you haven't finished your homework!

WENDY: But I can do my homework tomorrow! And then, Tim and Tom are coming, too.

FATHER: I don't care about Tim and Tom. Stop talking about these boys. You spend too much time with them.

WENDY: But we always have a lot of fun together.

FATHER: Fun isn't everything! Do you remember what you promised us after you had shown us your bad school report last year?

WENDY: Alright. But I have been working all afternoon, and I would go on if this concert wasn't taking place tonight.

FATHER: Okay, you may go today, but you must do your homework tomorrow!

Vorsicht beim Übersetzen: Im Deutschen musst du in der indirekten Rede den **Konjunktiv** anstelle des Indikativs der wörtlichen Rede verwenden, im Englischen steht dagegen eine andere **Zeitform des Verbs**!

Beispiel: Er sagte: „Ich bin glücklich, dass ich in die Disko gegangen bin."
Er sagte, er sei glücklich, dass er in die Disko gegangen sei.
He said: "I am happy that I went to the disco."
He said he was happy that he had gone to the disco.

ufgabe 6 Translate.

Als mein Vater mich gestern Abend fragte, warum ich die ganze Zeit so fröhlich sei, sagte ich ihm, dass ich eine gute Nachricht bekommen hätte. Natürlich wollte er wissen, was los sei. Ich erzählte ihm, dass ich am darauf folgenden Wochenende mit sieben Mädchen und Jungen aus meiner Klasse Zelten gehen würde. Ich sah, dass er mich fragen wollte, warum ich es ihm nicht früher gesagt habe, aber dann stellte er diese Frage nicht, sondern sagte mir, ich solle möglichst bald meine Sachen für das Wochenende packen. Er fügte hinzu, dass er drei von uns mit dem Auto zum Bahnhof bringen könne, damit wir nicht alles selbst tragen müssten. Natürlich sagte ich nicht nein!

Aufgabe 7* **Mixed exercise:** Restore the dialogue by changing reported speech back into direct speech. Of course, you can also do this exercise the other way round, by starting with the solution (p. 227) and turning it into reported speech.

One evening, at a comprehensive school, Mr Smith spoke to parents and teachers about young criminals. After his speech, some parents – and some teachers, too – asked him questions, and he gave answers. The next day, he tells his wife about this discussion.

"One mother wanted to know what her husband and she could do if they found out that their daughter had stolen something from a supermarket. I told her to give the things back, talk to her and try to solve her problems, because she wouldn't steal if she had no problems.
Another mother asked me what I would do if my child broke into a house. I said I didn't really know, that I hoped the atmosphere in our family was good enough that my children would never become criminals.
A teacher remarked that I had been talking about children of 10 to 16 years, and wondered what happened to older youngsters. I explained to him that there were the same sentences for young offenders between 17 and 20, but more of them were sent to special prisons.
One father wanted to know if I had any suggestions about how crime was best prevented. I had to admit that I was afraid the only thing we could do was to show children that they didn't have to have everything they saw!
The teacher asked, too, whether the government wouldn't have to do something about it if there were more and more young criminals, and I told him that I agreed with him, but I also pointed out that they had done a lot already. Still, I added, more had to be done to help families to give their children enough care and love.
One of the mothers broke down in tears and explained that she would never have thought that her 8-year-old son would steal something, but the day before she had wanted to pay at the greengrocer's and had found out that twenty pounds had been missing from her purse. She asked whether she should punish him or whether it was enough to talk to him. I said she didn't really have to punish him, but she should make sure that he understood what he had done, and that she understood why he had done it."

Tipps zum *dialogue writing*

In der folgenden Aufgabe sollst du auf Englisch einen Dialog schreiben. Du bekommst in diesem Fall ziemlich genaue Angaben darüber, was die Personen sagen sollen; bei anderen Aufgaben wird dir vielleicht nur das Thema des Gesprächs vorgegeben und du musst noch viel mehr selbst erfinden. In jedem Fall solltest du ein paar Dinge beachten:

- Ein Dialog muss lebendig sein. Um das zu erreichen, solltest du **Ausrufe** (z. B. *Oh dear! Not really! That's not true!*), kurze **Fragen** und **Rückfragen** (z. B. *Really? Tell me more! Do they?*), *question tags* (z. B. *…, isn't it?*) und Füllwörter (z. B. *well, you know*) verwenden.
- Ein Dialog ist keine Geschichte. Du darfst ruhig **kürzere Sätze** schreiben.
- Ein Dialog vollzieht sich **spontan**. Die Gesprächspartner dürfen sich z. B. auch einmal gegenseitig unterbrechen.
- Ein Dialog braucht einen **Anfang** (Begrüßung) und einen **Schluss** (Verabschiedung, z. B. mit Verabredung zu einem Treffen).
- **Verwende ganz normales Englisch**; versuche nicht, viele besonders ausgefallene Wörter zu benutzen – im alltäglichen Gespräch tut das niemand!

Aufgabe 8

a) Dialogue writing. Do not translate the German indications on the right, but express the underlined passages in English.

S: Hi, Tom!	Sarah trifft ihren Mitschüler Tom im Pausenhof und spricht ihn an.
S:	Da sich Tom mürrisch abwendet, ohne zu antworten, läuft Sarah ihm nach und fragt ihn, was los ist.
T: S:	Tom gibt eine ausweichende Antwort, aber Sarah lässt nicht locker. Irgendetwas muss ja passiert sein.
T:	Tom rückt endlich mit der Sprache heraus: Sein Fußballteam hat am Vortag verloren.
S:	Sarah meint, das sei doch nicht so schlimm.
T:	Da protestiert Tom: Erstens ist ihre Schule jetzt seit zwölf Jahren zum ersten Mal nicht beim Stadtfinale dabei und zweitens ist er an der Niederlage schuld.
S:	Natürlich will Sarah wissen, warum.
T:	Tom erzählt, dass es kurz vor Schluss noch 0:0 stand und dass die Gegner durch einen Fehlpass von ihm das entscheidende Tor schießen konnten.

S: Sarah versucht Tom zu trösten: der Torhüter hätte den Ball ja auch noch halten können!

T: Aber Tom will das nicht akzeptieren, wirft Sarah vor, sie verstehe ja doch nichts von Fußball und läuft davon.

S: Sarah ruft ihm zwar noch nach, aber dann denkt sie sich ihren Teil und geht wieder ins Schulhaus.

b) During lunch hour, Sarah tells her best friend Tina about her conversation with Tom. Turn the dialogue into reported speech. Use different reporting verbs. Start like this:

"I said hello to Tom, but he didn't seem to hear me. So I asked him what the matter was and what I ______ "

14 Schwierige Aufgaben zum Knobeln

ufgabe 1 A Homophone Crossword: Put in words which sound the same, but are written differently.

Across: 1 knight, 4 sites, 8 here, 10 deer, 11 flour, 14 I, 15 so, 17 see, 18 scene, 19 by, 20 board, 21 blew, 22 new

Down: 1 know, 2 guest, 3 through, 4 sail, 5 whole, 6 too, 7 hour, 9 bee, 11 four, 12 wear, 13 knows, 16 buy, 17 sun

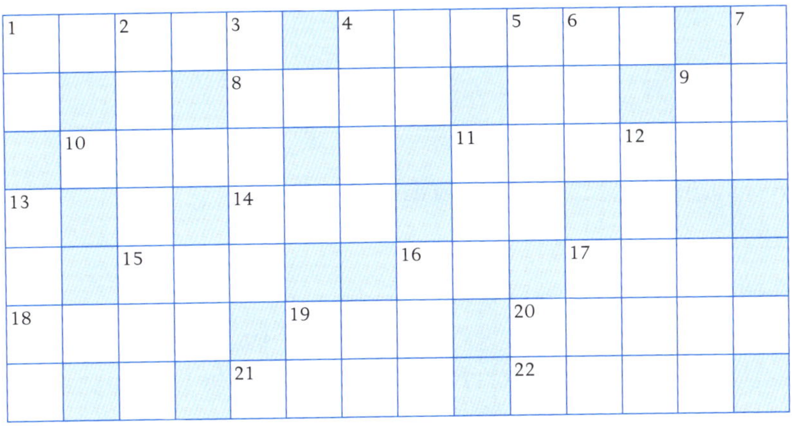

To help you, here are definitions for the words you have to put in – but you must complete them.

Across

1 The hours ________________ follow the day.
4 ________________ you are in another city, you want to see them.
8 ________________ do this, you need your ears.
10 This is the word you start a letter to a friend ________________
11 It won't grow well ________________ it isn't watered properly.
14 You ________________ see with it.
15 You do this ________________ a needle and thread.
17 It's all made ________________ water.
18 Past ________________ of *to see.*
19 You must do it when you need ________________ food, for example.
20 The opposite ________________ interested.
21 ________________ colour.
22 Second form of an ________________ verb.

Down

1 If you don't want to do something, you ________________ it.
2 You did it when you didn't really know one of the words in this crossword ________________
3 You did it with ________________ ball.
4 When a lot of things ________________ sold.
5 When it's in a bucket, water can run ________________ it.
6 ________________ number.
7 Possessive ________________ (not pronoun!).
9 This verb can be a full verb and an ________________
11 ________________ preposition.
12 A question ________________
13 You need it ________________ smelling things.
16 You say it when you leave ________________
17 A child, but ________________ a daughter.

Aufgabe 2 Use the right past tenses for the verbs in brackets.

The Smiths ________________ 1 (arrive) in Key West for their holidays. They ________________ 2 (never be) there before, and it's the first time they are going to spend a holiday at the seaside. While Mr Smith ________________ 3 (read) his newspaper four months ago, he suddenly ________________ 4 (see) a report on Key West. He ________________ 5 (like) the town at once, so they ________________ 6 (book) rooms at a hotel the following day. They ________________ 7 (not want) to write a letter, but it ________________ 8 (be) very difficult to get through by telephone, because a lot of people ________________ 9 (try) to ring up that hotel. But at last Mr Smith ________________ 10 (manage) to get three nice rooms. On the day of their arrival, in the afternoon, they want to go for a walk.

MRS SMITH: Why ________________ 11 (you/not put) on a pullover, Jim? It's cold today.

JIM: Well, I, er, because I ________________ 12 (not bring) one. I ________________ 13 (not pack) my red one yesterday, because I don't really like it, and I ________________ 14 (not can) find my blue one.

MRS SMITH: Why ________________ 15 (you/not ask) me to buy a new pullover for you when I ________________ 16 (go) to the city centre last week? ________________ 17 (you/hear) that I ________________ 18 (go),

	________[19] (you/not)? By the way, what ________[20] (you/do) when I ________[21] (leave) the house that day?
JIM:	I don't remember. But I know at least that I ________[22] (not listen) to records because I ________[23] (take) my record-player to be repaired two days before, and I ________ ________[24] (not get) it back yet. I ________[25] (try) to repair it myself for several hours, but in the end I ________[26] (must) give up.
MR SMITH:	Well, we all know that you aren't very good at repairing things! Do you remember what ________[27] (happen) when you ________[28] (try) to repair the dishwasher?
JACKY:	Don't remind me of that! He ________[29] (hammer) and ________[30] (turn) screws when suddenly the big flood ________[31] (come). How fast you ________[32] (run) away, Jim!
JIM:	Alright, alright! But at least I ________[33] (make) an attempt! Before I ________[34] (do), you ________[35] (not even look) at the instruction manual to find out what ________[36] (be) wrong.
MRS SMITH:	Now don't spoil our holidays with those old stories. Can we start our walk now? I really want to see the house Ernest Hemingway ________[37] (live) in! I ________[38] (hear) so much about it. ________[39] (you/read) the leaflet I ________[40] (give) you about it, honey?
MR SMITH:	No, I ________[41] (do). But I'm sure you ________[42] (learn) everything by heart, so you can tell us now.
MRS SMITH:	Don't tease me. But it seems that I'm really the only one in our family who ________[43] (prepare) herself a bit for these holidays. I ________[44] (read) about things since Christmas!

Aufgabe 3 Ask the party guests' questions.

Aufgabe 4 Have a look again at the dialogues in exercise 3. Turn them into reported speech.

a) Andy asked Lizzy ____________________

b) ____________________

c) ____________________

d) ____________________

e) ____________________

f) ____________________

g) ____________________

h) ____________________

Aufgabe 5 Gerund, participle or infinitive? Choose the right forms of the verbs in brackets and change the underlined passages, using participles or infinitives. Add prepositions where necessary.

A man ____________[1] (call) Buffalo Bill

William Frederick Cody, who was born[2] in 1846, became one of the most famous showmen who travelled[3] through the Wild West. His first profession was ____________[4] (hunt) buffalo, and after his ____________[5] (shoot) 4 280 bison in 17 months for the workers of the Kansas railroad, people started ____________[6] (call) this sure-____________[7] (aim) and well-____________[8] (train) hunter 'Buffalo Bill', as it was the custom in those times ____________[9] (give) people nicknames.

____________[10] (entertain) the Americans at the East coast, some people had had the idea ____________[11] (start) Wild West Shows, which should show[12] them what life in the West was like. The shows were designed ____________[13] (make) life there look like a glorious adventure, and when one of these shows came to a town, nobody wanted ____________[14] (miss) ____________[15] (see) it.

Today we aren't able ____________[16] (imagine) how people really lived out in the West at that time. ____________[17] (be) in the West meant ____________[18] (have) to live a hard life. Imagine ____________[19] (sleep) under the stars! And what about ____________[20] (live) in the constant danger ____________[21] (be) attacked by Indians or bandits?

Would you have liked ______________________[22] (be) a pioneer who hunted[23] buffalo to have something ____________________[24] (eat)?
Anyway, W. F. Cody, ____________________[25] (name) 'Buffalo Bill' by his fellow pioneers, one day met 'Wild Bill' Hickok, who was one of the stars in a Wild West Show. Hickok really wanted Cody ____________________[26] (join) his show, and in the end he agreed ________________________[27] (do) so.
It wasn't difficult for Buffalo Bill ____________________[28] (present) his abilities to the public. But after ______________________[29] (act) and ______________[30] (play) for some time, he became tired ____________________[31] (work) for others and started ____________________[32] (wonder) about how ______________[33] (continue) his life. Instead ____________________[34] (be) dependent on others, he preferred ________________________[35] (become) his own boss, but he knew that ______________________[36] (start) a show of his own wouldn't be an easy task for him ________________________[37] (perform); at last, however, he was sure that it would be worth ______________________[38] (try).
So, in 1883, he was at last bold enough ______________[39] (try) ______________[40] (create) his own "Buffalo Bill's Wild West Show", a spectacular circus that toured[41] the United States, and it starred[42], among others, Annie Oakley and Sitting Bull.
His became the best__________________[43] (know) show in the US, and nobody ever regretted __________________[44] (buy) a ticket and ____________________[45] (see) the show. Even former pioneers and settlers who knew what the West was really like, didn't mind ____________________[46] (watch): it reminded them ______________[47] (ride) horses, and they remembered ______________[48] (smell) the air of the wilderness. And Buffalo Bull remembered (put) ____________[49] everything into his show that might attract a lot of people. When he came to Europe, his show didn't need ________________[50] (advertise): everybody there had long waited for Buffalo Bill ______________[51] (come) to the old world. By the time Cody died in 1917, his show had become the greatest show of its time ______________________[52] (tour) the whole world.

ufgabe 6 Do you remember Mr Smith, the expert on crime and especially on young criminals (p. 162)? Here is the speech he prepared for the evening with parents of a Birmingham comprehensive.

... Of course, we cannot treat young offenders the same way we treat adult criminals. Courts do not send children to prison with grown-ups (although I must say that the British government made prison a possibility for 12- to 14-year-olds in October 1994), but sometimes they must pass a strict sentence.
Authorities bring young offenders between 10 and 16 before a special court. In the past, they gave these courts the name 'juvenile court', but since 1992, they have called them 'youth courts'. The government changed other details in 1992, too, but we needn't discuss these details here. We are only talking about the most important things today.
If the court finds a child guilty, it will order him to pay for the damage he has done or will make him pay a fine. Another possibility is ordering that a social worker supervise the child for some time. For very serious crimes, however, the court may order imprisonment in a place which the Home Secretary agrees to ...

Before he starts his speech, Mr Smith remembers that the passive voice sounds much more official and impersonal. Write down what he tells the parents in the end:

... Of course, young offenders cannot be treated the same way ...

Aufgabe 7 A comprehension test about Abraham Lincoln: Read the text carefully, then answer the questions, using relative clauses.

People of the United States see Abraham Lincoln as one of the greatest leaders in the history of their country. Every year many thousands of Americans visit the great white marble Lincoln Memorial in Washington, D. C.; they have put his likeness on their money and their stamps.

Lincoln was born in 1809 in the American state of Kentucky. Living conditions were dangerous and difficult. Schools were few and generally bad. Lincoln was born into a family of poor farmers. He himself worked on the family farm until 1831. During his whole life he had less than one year of formal education. But he worked hard, and in the end he became one of the most learned men of his time.

Lincoln was also known and respected for many other qualities, such as fairness and honesty. As a lawyer, he agreed to defend people in court only when their cases were right and just in his eyes.

Lincoln became President of the United States at the moment of the nation's greatest crisis since 1776, when 13 American colonies had declared their independence from Great Britain; with them the real history of the United States had begun.

Despite Lincoln's efforts, war came: Civil War, a war between the states; fathers fought sons, brothers fought brothers; the war caused terrible bloodshed and almost destroyed the nation.

By the end of Lincoln's presidency, slavery had been ended forever in the nation; peace came on April 9, 1865, and everybody hoped for a new and happier life. But for Lincoln that new and happier life did not last long. On April 14, 1865, he was shot while sitting in a theater in Washington, D. C., together with his wife. The next day he was dead; his influence and importance, however, were to live long after he had gone to rest in his grave.

a) Who was Abraham Lincoln?

Abraham Lincoln is the man *(who/whom/that) people of the United States see as one of the greatest leaders in the history of their country.*

b) What is the Lincoln Memorial?

The Lincoln Memorial is the place ______________________________

c) What has Kentucky got to do with Abraham Lincoln?

____

d) Who were poor farmers?

____

e) Why is the year 1831 important for the life of Abraham Lincoln?

____

f) What other qualities was Lincoln known for?

____

g) Who did he only defend in court?

____

h) At what moment did Lincoln become President?

____

i) With whom had the real history of the United States begun?

____

j) Describe the Civil War.

____

k) What seems most important in Lincoln's presidency today?

____

l) Could Lincoln enjoy peace?

____

m) What did Lincoln do in the last few hours of his life?

____

n) What does everybody agree upon?

____

Aufgabe 8 Abraham Lincoln again! Put in the correct tenses.

a) When Americans ____________________ (think) of Abraham Lincoln, they ____________________ (see) him as one of the greatest leaders in the history of their country.

b) If Lincoln ____________________ (not be) liked so very much by Americans, they ____________________________ (not visit) the Lincoln Memorial by the thousands every year.

c) Americans ________________ (not put) his likeness on their money and their stamps if he ________________ (not do) so many important things.

d) If Lincoln ________________ (be) born into another family, he ________________ (perhaps have) an easier start into life.

e) He ________________ (can go) to school longer if more and better schools ________________ (exist).

f) Lincoln ________________ (not become) a famous and respected lawyer if he ________________ (not work) hard throughout his life.

g) If he ________________ (not have) all his other qualities, he ________________ (not be) so respected even today.

h) As a lawyer, he used to say to people who were seeking his advice: "I ________________ (only defend) you in court if your case ________________ (be) really right and just!"

i) If the northern states ________________ (not already abolish) slavery, the Civil War ________________ (not happen).

j) In addition, the war ________________ (can be) avoided if the Southern states ________________ (not separate) from the North.

k) When Lincoln's friends ________________ (ask) him about ending the war, he ________________ (use) to say: "I ________________ (must) accept slavery in the South, if only the nation ________________ (can be) united again!"

l) Lincoln ________________ (certainly do) a lot of other good deeds if he ________________ (not be) shot in 1865.

m) If slavery ________________ (still exist) today, all of Lincoln's efforts ________________ (be) in vain.

n) But if Lincoln ________________ (live) today, he certainly ________________ (not be) happy about the situation of the Blacks in the United States.

o) It ________________ (only change) if politicians ________________ (dare) to really help the minorities in their country at last.

fgabe 9 In the following text about Walt Disney, every fifth word is missing. Find suitable words to fill in the blanks. Of course, sometimes several solutions are possible, but only one is ideal. To help you, the first letter of each word is already there.

Walt Disney's name is k______[1] around the world, but e______[2] better known are all t______[3] characters which were created b______[4] him: Mickey Mouse, Donald D______[5], Goofy, and countless others. A______[6] Disney is world-famous for b______[7] a cartoonist, a showman, a______[8] a businessman, he was m______[9] a storyteller. Disney once s______[10] of his work: "Every g______[11] play has a lesson t______[12] teach. That's why writers h______[13] always insisted the stage – a______[14] now the screen – is t______[15] and effectively a moral f______[16]. What's the sense of m______[17] a picture unless you h______[18] something important to say? T______[19] trick is to say i______[20] without preaching."

Walt Disney w______[21] born in Chicago, Illinois, i______[22] 1901. At the age o______[23] five, his family moved t______[24] a farm in Missouri, w______[25] Walt drew sketches of t______[26] barnyard creatures and the s______[27] he saw around the f______[28]. In 1910, his father s______[29] the farm and moved t______[30] family to Kansas, where h______[31] bought a newspaper delivery b______[32], in which Walt and h______[33] brother Roy helped a l______[34]. Later, during the First W______[35] War, Walt served as a______[36] ambulance driver for the R______[37] Cross. In 1923, after h______[38] produced his first animated c______[39], Walt went to California i______[40] order to start a n______[41] company there, the Disney S______[42]. In addition to all t______[43] cartoons starring Mickey and m______[44] others, Disney also worked o______[45] new animated films in w______[46] music and cartoon animation j______[47] together in telling a s______[48]. Later films mixed real a______[49] with cartoon characters. In t______[50] 1950s, Walt Disney began w______[51] in other areas of e______[52], too. He started to g______[53] more serious attention to n______[53] films and live action f______[54]. He also began a l______[55]-running TV series, and h______[56] opened his first amusement p______[57], Disneyland. All this work b______[58] by Walt Disney continues t______[59], long after his death. A______[60] learning from his doctors i______[61] October 1966 that he w______[62] suffering from cancer, Disney h______[63] one of his lungs t______[64] out. Nevertheless, he died o______[65] December 15 of the s______[66] year in a hospital d______[67] across the street from h______[68] studio.

15 Schwierige Wörter, die wir in diesem Buch benutzen

ability – Fähigkeit
(to) accompany s.b. – jdn. begleiten
acquaintance – Bekannter
advice – Ratschlag
anchor – Anker
ancient – alt
annex – Anbau
apprentice – Lehrling
attempt – Versuch
(to) attend (a school) – (eine Schule) besuchen
au pair – Au-pair(-Mädchen)

bank clerk – Bankangestellter
barnyard – Bauernhof
bloke (infm.) – Kerl
bloodshed – Blutvergießen
bold – tapfer
boot – Kofferraum
(to be a) bore – (ein) Langweiler (sein)
bottle bank – Altglascontainer
brave – mutig
(to) bury – begraben

can bank – Container für leere Dosen
(to) cancel – absagen
cancer – Krebs
(to) capture – gefangen nehmen
chase – Jagd
cheerful – fröhlich
chess – Schach
clockwise – im Uhrzeigersinn
competition – Wettbewerb
(to) consider – betrachten
constantly – dauernd

countless – unzählig
court – Gerichtshof

(to) **d**are – wagen
decade – Jahrzehnt
(to) defeat – besiegen
(to) defend – verteidigen
(to) deliver a speech – eine Rede halten
(to) deteriorate – sich verschlechtern
disappointed – enttäuscht
disguise – Verkleidung
(to) disturb – stören

ecstatic – ausgelassen
effort – Anstrengung
emperor – Kaiser
entrance – Eingang
environmentalist – Umweltschützer
exhibition – Ausstellung
(to) extend – erweitern

(to) **f**ail – keinen Erfolg haben
(to) favor *(AE)*, favour *(BE)* – bevorzugen
(to) fell – fällen
flock – Herde
fortnight – vierzehn Tage
foundation – Stiftung
French fries – Pommes frites
fuel – Treibstoff

(to) **g**amble – spielen (Glücksspiel)
gifted – begabt
grave – Grab
(to) guide – führen
guide – Führer
gymnasium – Turnhalle

habit – Gewohnheit
hairdresser's – Frisörladen
handlebars – Fahrradlenker
haughty – hochnäsig
(to) head – an der Spitze stehen
herbs – Kräuter

Home Secretary *(BE)* – Innenminister
honesty – Ehrlichkeit
(to) honor *(AE)*, honour *(BE)* – ehren
hostage – Geisel
hubcap – Radkappe

identical – identisch, gleich
incredible – unglaublich
indeed – in der Tat
independence – Unabhängigkeit
independent – unabhängig
(to) inhabit – bewohnen
(to) insist – bestehen auf
interpreter – Dolmetscher
(to) introduce – vorstellen
invaluable – unbezahlbar
invention – Erfindung
iron – Eisen, Bügeleisen

juvenile – jugendlich

(to) **k**night – zum Ritter schlagen

landmark – Wahrzeichen
lawyer – Rechtsanwalt
light bulb – Glühbirne
likeness – Konterfei
litter – Abfall
living conditions – Lebensbedingungen

marble – Marmor
meanwhile – mittlerweile, inzwischen
(to) mention – erwähnen
metal fatigue – hier: Materialermüdung
minority – Minderheit

nickname – Spitzname

(to be) **o**bliged to	–	verpflichtet sein zu
(to) occupy	–	besetzen
offender	–	Straftäter
opponent	–	Gegner
outskirts	–	Vororte
(to) **p**ass sth. on	–	etwas weitergeben
pigeon	–	Taube
pattern	–	Muster
(to) pay a visit	–	einen Besuch abstatten
peak	–	Gipfel, Höhepunkt
pedestrian	–	Fußgänger
penalty	–	Strafe
performance	–	Vorstellung
permanent	–	andauernd
(to) persuade	–	überzeugen
pigeon	–	Taube
pity	–	Mitleid
(to) pollute	–	verschmutzen
precious	–	wertvoll
(to) prevent	–	verhüten
progress	–	Fortschritt
prohibition	–	Verbot
purchase	–	Kauf
(to) **q**uarrel	–	streiten
(to) queue	–	Schlange stehen
(to) **r**ain cats and dogs	–	wie aus Kübeln regnen
(to) recapture	–	wieder einfangen
(to) recover	–	sich erholen
(to) reign	–	regieren, herrschen
relieved	–	erleichtert
(to) rely on	–	sich verlassen auf
(to) retreat	–	sich zurückziehen
riddle	–	Rätsel
road sweeper	–	Straßenkehrer
(the) Roman Empire	–	das Römische Reich
rubber	–	Gummi
seagull	–	Seemöwe
(to) seek	–	suchen

sentence – hier: Strafe
(to) serve – dienen
several – mehrere
(to) sew – nähen
similar – ähnlich
skilful – geschickt
slavery – Sklaverei
spectator – Zuschauer
speech – Rede
(to) star – jdn. zum Hauptdarsteller haben
steep – steil
(to) struggle – kämpfen
subway – Fußgängerunterführung *(BE)*, U-Bahn *(AE)*
(to) suffer – leiden
(to) suppose – annehmen

(to) **t**ear – ziehen, reißen
(to) tidy (up) – aufräumen
tightrope – Drahtseil
(to) treat – behandeln
treaty – Vertrag
(to) tremble – zittern
triangle – Dreieck
tribe – Stamm

unless – wenn nicht
upright – aufrecht

in **v**ain – vergeblich
vehicle – Fahrzeug
vicious – böse
voluntary organisation – karitative Hilfsorganisation
voyage – Seereise

(to) **w**aste – verschwenden
wardrobe – Kleiderschrank
warrior – Krieger
weapon – Waffe
Whitsun – Pfingsten
(to) wound – verwunden

zealous – eifrig

Lösungen

Bestimmte und unbestimmte Artikel

Aufgabe 1

a) Sandy is on her way to school. She thinks: "I hope I will meet Lisa today."

b) In Broad Street, she really/actually meets her friend, who spent her holidays at Lake Michigan.

c) Lisa says that she was in New York, too, and saw the Empire State Building, the East River and Broadway there. (She was also in New York.)

Aufgabe 2

[1]–, [2]the, [3]–, [4]–, [5]the, [6]the, [7]the, [8]–, [9]–, [10]the, [11]–, [12]–, [13]the, [14]the, [15]–, [16]–, [17]–, [18]the, [19]the, [20]–, [21]The, [22]the, [23]the, [24]the, [25]–, [26]the, [27]–,[28]the, [29]the, [30]–, [31]–, [32]the, [33]the

Aufgabe 3

[1]a boy, [2]a girl, [3]an Indian, [4]a Navajo, [5]a miner, [6]boss of the mining company, [7]a White, [8]a Protestant, [9]an excellent cook, [10]a good story-teller, [11]three times a day, [12]a present, [13]a pair

Aufgabe 4

a) The, a, –, –

b) the, –

c) the

d) the, a

e) the, the, the, –/the

f) a, –

g) a, the, –/the, –

h) –/the, –, a

i) the

j) the, the, –

k) an/–

l) the, –, –, a

m) the, the, a, –

n) the, Answer: Thomas often goes to the cinema in London.

o) the, Answer: The architect designs his houses in San Francisco.

name	town	hobby	parents' profession
Thomas	London	cinema	museum guide
Sabine	Luxemburg	stamps	bus driver
Roy	San Francisco	climbing	architect
Patricia	New York	swimming	bank clerk
Maria	Rio de Janeiro	biking	hotel manageress

Pronomen und Begleiter

Aufgabe 1 [1]I, [2]It, [3]it, [4]he, [5]her, [6]you, [7]me, [8]She, [9]me, [10]you, [11]I, [12]they, [13]you, [14]them, [15]We, [16]they, [17]you, [18]us, [19]you, [20]them, [21]him, [22]he

Aufgabe 2

a) Is this your school-bag? It's very nice. May I take it?

b) Where are Peter and Francis? Do you see them? Oh, there they are!

c) Do you often go for a walk here? I have never seen you before.

d) May I introduce you? This is Cecilia. You haven't met her yet; she's my cousin from Canada.

Aufgabe 3

a) Is your classroom on the first floor, Mrs Price?

b) My children are (just) doing their homework.

c) Give this pocket calculator to my sister, please; it's hers. You can tell her that I'm going to give her her book tomorrow.

d) You can't leave the classroom just like that!

e) The gymnasium and the stairs which lead to it are very dirty today, but most of the time our school and its surroundings are completely clean.

Aufgabe 4 [1]yours, [2]my, [3]mine, [4]hers, [5]her, [6]her/its, [7]ours, [8]Our, [9]our/their, [10]hers, [11]yours, [12]your, [13]theirs, [14]yours fgabe 5 Many/A lot of German pupils/students can't imagine that English schools differ widely from German ones. Only somebody who is at a school in England for some time will be able to enjoy himself there. Anyway, he will remember for a long time everything that is different in England. For example, in some schools pupils stand up when the teacher enters the classroom, and in the morning it is the headteacher himself who welcomes the pupils.

fgabe 6
a) ... looking at each other.
b) ... is cleaning itself.
c) ... are buying each other presents.
d) ... are helping each other with their homework.
e) ... is teaching herself Russian.
f) ... are carrying each other's school-bags.

fgabe 7*

YOU:	Hi, Dorothy.	Begrüßung
DOROTHY:	Hi, ... How are you?	
YOU:	I'm fine, thanks. And you?	
DOROTHY:	I'm fine, too. You know, I like staying here a lot. But what are you doing with that microphone?	
YOU:	Well, I'd like to interview you for our school magazine. You know, the other pupils want to know something about schools in Great Britain. Is that okay?	Hinführung zum Interview Erklärung Einverständnis erfragen
DOROTHY:	Yes, of course. Go ahead with your questions. Or do you want me to talk just like that?	
YOU:	Well, just as you please. Most of all, we want to know what is different at your school.	
Dorothy:	Oh, there's a lot. First of all, morning classes start at 9, and we have Assembly first.	
YOU:	What's that?	Zwischenfragen
DOROTHY:	All the pupils come together, the teachers find out if somebody is ill, and the headteacher tells us important things.	
YOU:	But school isn't over at one o'clock then, is it?	„question tags“

DOROTHY: Of course not. We often have school in the afternoon, sometimes until five. But there is lunch, too: one hour in which we can go home or have lunch at the school cafeteria.

YOU: We haven't got a cafeteria. So you can have warm meals at school?

Vergleich mit eigener Schule

DOROTHY: Yes, and sometimes they're quite good!

YOU: What about homework? You get home rather late, don't you?

DOROTHY: Yes, we do, but we've got homework to do even so.

YOU: Oh dear!

Ausrufe

DOROTHY: I think one more big difference is that primary school starts at age 5 already and that A-levels are at age 18, after sixth form.

YOU: 'A-levels', 'sixth form'? What's that? I've never heard of that before!

Nicht Verstandenes erfragen

DOROTHY: I think you call it 'Abitur'. It's not exactly the same, but you need it if you want to go to university. And 'sixth form' is the name for the last two years before A-levels.

YOU: I see. Now I've got one more question. I've heard a lot about Eton – Prince William went there, didn't he? What's that?

DOROTHY: Oh, you know a lot! Well, Eton is one of the best-known public schools. You know, I go to a state-run school, but Eton is for rich people who can pay a lot of money for their children's education.

YOU: So 'public schools' are really private ones?

DOROTHY: Yes, that's true.

Dank und Verabschiedung

YOU: Thank you, Dorothy. I think I can write a long article now. Bye!

DOROTHY: You're welcome. See you tomorrow!

Aufgabe 8 [1]anybody/anyone, [2]anywhere, [3]somewhere, [4]anybody/anyone, [5]somebody/someone, [6]any, [7]some, [8]sometimes, [9]somebody/someone, [10]somewhere, [11]anybody/anyone, [12]Some fgabe 9 [1]all, [2]each, [3]everything, [4]any, [5]each, [6]each, [7]all, [8]anything, [9]all, [10]each

gabe 10 [1]a lot of/much, [2]a lot of, [3]a lot of/many, [4]few/fewer, [5]little/less, [6]few, [7]a lot of/many, [8]a lot of, [9]little/less

gabe 11 [1]all/everything, [2]a lot, [3]few, [4]many/a lot, [5]some/many/most, [6]fewer, [7]some/a little, [8]little, [9]more/anything/everything, [10]somebody/someone, [11]a few/some, [12]much, [13]some/a little, [14]nothing/little, [15]less, [16]None, [17]something/somehow, [18]No

gabe 12*

- … We didn't know each other …
- … so we introduced each other/told each other our names.
- … sat down …
- … so did Carol.
- … Chris and I looked at each other, …
- … neither Chris nor me …
- … both/either of them …
- "Neither do I."
- "I do, though!"
- … both/either of them.
- … neither of us answered.
- … I remembered …
- … them both/both of them.
- … I must hurry.
- … we saw each other/we met.

gabe 13*

S	H	E	V	E	R	Y	B	O	D	Y	O	U	R	S	O	M	E
1		2								3				4			5

A	C	H	I	M	I	N	E	A	C	H	E	R	S	O	M	E
		6		7			8			9			10			

B	O	D	Y	O	U	S	O	U	R	S	O	M	E	H	O	W	E	I	T	H	E	R
			11		12	13	14			15						16	17					

S	U	C	C	E	S	S

Adjektive

Aufgabe 1

high, low
glad, sad
soft, hard
different, similar
easy, difficult
far, near
bad, **skilful**
interesting, boring
ugly, beautiful
heavy, light
new, old
slow, fast
slim, fat

Aufgabe 2

fat, heavy, ugly, old, boring, difficult, slow, far, slim, light, beautiful, new, interesting, easy, fast, near

Aufgabe 3

a) late
b) rich, poor
c) silly, silly
d) gifted
e) hot
f) golden
g) dead
h) English
i) Old
j) Empty
k) longest
l) best, worst
m) best, best
n) greener
o) First, first

Aufgabe 4

a) The World Trade Center was the highest building in New York; it was higher than all the others.
b) Broadway is the longest street in New York; it's longer than all the others.
c) Grand Central Station is the biggest (railway/train) station in New York; it's bigger than all the others.
d) Times Square is the most interesting square in New York; it's more interesting than all the others.
e) Madame Tussaud's is the most exciting museum in London; it's more exciting than all the others.

f) Piccadilly Circus is the busiest place in London; it's busier than all the others.

g) Westminster Abbey is the most important church in London; it's more important than all the others.

h) Big Ben is the most famous tower in London; it's more famous than all the others.

ufgabe 5
a) It's absolutely necessary that the rich help the poor.
b) The Dutch live in the Netherlands./The French live in France.
c) Everybody likes friendly waitresses better than unfriendly waitresses.
d) The young of today will be the old of tomorrow.
e) The English and the Germans have not always lived together peacefully.

ufgabe 6
a) Jim wears nicer shoes, but Joe wears bigger ones.
b) Jim wears cleaner clothes, but Joe wears more elegant ones.
c) Jim drives a faster car, but Joe drives a more expensive one.
d) Jim carries heavier parcels, but Joe carries larger ones.
e) Jim paints more beautiful pictures, but Joe paints more interesting ones.
f) Jim has a happier face, but Joe has a more intelligent one.

Adverbien

ufgabe 1
quickly, hard, easily, excellently, well, Happily, in a friendly way

ufgabe 2
a) **Last Saturday,** we drove to a soccer match **in Liverpool**. / We drove to a soccer match **in Liverpool last Saturday**.

b) **Unfortunately,** the train was **very** full. / The train was **very** full, **unfortunately**.

c) **Usually** it is empty, but **probably that day** everything was different because of the match. / It is **usually** empty, but **probably that day** everything was different because of the match. / …, but **probably** everything was different **that day** because of the match.

d) When we **finally** arrived **in Liverpool**, we couldn't **even** get off the train **at once**.

e) So we **angrily** waited until the other passengers had got off **at last**. / So we waited **angrily** until the other passengers had got off **at last**. / … until the other passengers had **at last** got off.

f) **Luckily,** we arrived **at the stadium before 4 o'clock**.

g) We went in **happily**, and the match started **immediately**. / We went in **happily**, and **immediately** the match started.

h) When we went back **to the station two hours later**, we all shouted **cheerfully**, because our team had won **gloriously**. / **Two hours later,** when we went back **to the station**, we all shouted **cheerfully**, because our team had won **gloriously**.

Aufgabe 3

a) In den letzten Wochen haben wir leider alle unsere Spiele deutlich verloren.

b) Natürlich hätten wir gerne besser gespielt, aber anscheinend spielen wir immer schlecht.

c) Hoffentlich enttäuschen wir unsere Anhänger nicht weiterhin so sehr.

d) Wenn doch, werden wir wahrscheinlich sehr bald viele unserer Anhänger verlieren.

Aufgabe 4

a) … faster than number fifteen.

b) Number nine swam more elegantly than number one.

c) Number three played more actively than number eight.

d) Number thirty-three rowed more powerfully than number twenty-one.

e) Number one practised harder than number seventeen.

f) Number eighty-eight ran more quickly than number seventy-four.

Aufgabe 5

[1]important, [2]badly, [3]fantastic, [4]unhappy, [5]really, [6]successful, [7]hard, [8]long, [9]easily, [10]well, [11]noisy, [12]ecstatically, [13]quickly, [14]incredible, [15]angry, [16]disappointed, [17]in an unfriendly way, [18]good, [19]invaluable, [20]nervously, [21]dear, [22]real, [23]absolutely, [24]successful, [25]successful

fgabe 6* Adjektive und Adverbien sind fett gedruckt

Good luck after all — Titel

Everything was **wonderful**! Harriet was looking forward to the hockey tournament in Birmingham, and she was **absolutely sure** she and her team had a **fair** chance to win it. For months, they had been practising **hard** two or three times a week, and their teacher, Mrs Morgan, was more **satisfied** with them from week to week.

anregende Einleitung

Vorgeschichte

On the Tuesday before the tournament, Harriet's parents had a **big** surprise for her: they gave her a **new** stick – and now Harriet knew they would win. But on the next day, while practising for the last time before that **important** weekend, something **terrible** happened: while **quickly** dribbling towards the goal with the ball, Harriet fell over her stick, and immediately her leg hurt **terribly**. She didn't want to cry, but the other girls saw at once that her leg was **a little** swollen, and so they took her to a **nearby** doctor's. Now Harriet was crying, of course: she was **afraid** she wouldn't be able to play in Birmingham. But **luckily**, the doctor told her that her leg was not broken. He gave her a prescription and advised her to stay in bed for two days.

Hauptteil

eigene Fortsetzung

In the end, Harriet was **lucky**. On Thursday already, her leg wasn't swollen any more, and on Saturday, Mrs Morgan allowed her to drive to Birmingham with the team. And on Sunday, Harriet was able to play from the **very** first minute, and she even scored three **fantastic** goals in her five matches. Her team was 'only' second in the end, but Harriet was **very** happy even so.

glückliches Ende

Zeiten der Vergangenheit

Aufgabe 1

	1/3 C	U	T		4 A	2 T	E			
	A					O		5/6 H	A	D
	M		7 W			R		E		
9 W	E	R	E		8/10 B	E	G	A	N	
			N		O			R		
	11/12 S	A	T		U			13 D	I	D
	T				G					
	O			14/17 T	H	O	U	15 G	H	16 T
18 F	O	R	G	O	T			A		O
	D			O				V		L
		19 W	O	K	E		20 R	E	A	D

Aufgabe 2 In their holidays, Rachel and Peter **were** in a hotel near a lake where they **were allowed to** go swimming every day. Of course, their mother **had to** be with them. They **tried** to get up early every day. Rachel always **wanted** to go surfing, but one day Peter **had** another idea. He **cycled** to a nearby village because there **was** a farm with beautiful horses there. From that day on, he **went** to the farm every morning, and he **stayed** there for two hours. Then he **rushed** back to the hotel, and later, he **had** breakfast with his sister and his mother. Sometimes, of course, they all **did** something together: they **climbed** a mountain or **flew** a kite. But on other days, they only **went** to the beach, **lay** down there and **read** a book or **talked** to each other or **did** nothing all day. The children really **enjoyed** their holidays!

Aufgabe 3 (Auch wenn du nur einen kurzen Brief schreibst, sollte doch die Einleitung nicht fehlen. Erst dann solltest du über den eigentlichen Grund für deinen Brief schreiben. Vergiss auch am Ende nicht Grüße und Grußformel!)

Dorothy Perkins	
20, Maid Marian Way	Hausnummer zuerst
Nottingham	
NG1 6GF	post code
Dear Dorothy,	Anrede
Thank you very much for your postcard from Spain.	Bezug auf früheren Kontakt
You must have had a lovely holiday! I didn't go so far away: I spent two weeks in Cornwall with my	Überleitung
brother and our parents, but it was great, too. We had excellent weather and the cottage we stayed in was fantastic. As the sun was shining all the time, we could do a lot of things. Of course, we went	eigene Erfahrung
swimming in the sea and lay on the beach – you should see my suntan! One day, we drove to Land's End, and we also visited a few castles, but I didn't	Empfänger ansprechen
find them very exciting – it's just old stones, isn't it? And in the evenings we all played games together. I'm sure you would have liked it, too.	Empfänger ansprechen
It's a pity you can't come and visit me next week, but I hope you can come to my birthday party in October; please write back soon to tell me if you have time.	zukünftige Kontakte ansprechen
Say hello to your sisters, and remember me to your parents. See you soon!	Grüße an Familie
Love, *Judy*	Schlussformel, Name

Aufgabe 4

a) "Did you take a ride to the top of the Empire State Building?"
"Yes, I did. I took a ride to the top of the Empire State Building."

b) "Did you try to get a ticket for a show on Broadway?"
"Yes, I did. I tried to get a ticket for a show on Broadway."

c) "Did you see a film in one of the cinemas round Times Square?"
"No, I didn't. I didn't see a film in one of the cinemas round Times Square."

d) "Did you visit one of the museums?"
"Yes, I did. I visited one of the museums."

e) "Did you go on a boat trip round Manhattan?"
"No, I didn't. I didn't go on a boat trip round Manhattan."

f) "Did you take a walk through Central Park?"
"Yes, I did. I took a walk through Central Park."

g) "Did you buy something/anything on 5th Avenue?"
"No, I didn't. I didn't buy anything on 5th Avenue."

h) "Did you ride one of the yellow taxis?"
"Yes, I did. I rode one of the yellow taxis."

i) "Did you look down from the Statue of Liberty?"
"Yes, I did. I looked down from the Statue of Liberty."

j) "Did you watch the planes at John F. Kennedy Airport?"
"No, I didn't. I didn't watch the planes at John F. Kennedy Airport."

k) "Did you book a cheap flight to another American city?"
"No, I didn't. I didn't book a cheap flight to another American city."

l) "Did you go to the outskirts by subway?"
"Yes, I did. I went to the outskirts by subway."

Aufgabe 5

a) [1]saw, [2]said, [3]didn't answer, [4]weren't, [5]was, [6]went, [7]could/was able to, [8]started, [9]came, [10]didn't go, [11]could/was allowed to, [12]couldn't/wasn't allowed to

b) Where did Peter see David?
What did he say to him?
Why didn't David answer?
What weren't they really after all?
Who was very angry?
Who(m) could he suddenly see?
Where did he start running to then?
When did Anne come?
Did they go home together?
How long could Anne stay? / How long was Anne allowed to stay?
Who couldn't stay so long? / Who wasn't allowed to stay so long?

ufgabe 6

a) Martin was cleaning/tidying his room.
b) Mrs Riley was sitting in the bathtub/was taking/having a bath.
c) Mr Riley was working in his/the garden.
d) Dick and Paul were playing a game.
e) Sooty was lying in bed.
f) Sally was watching TV.
g) Mickey and Mince were going upstairs.

ufgabe 7

[1]wasn't, [2]liked, [3]decided, [4]were already getting, [5]thought, [6]won, [7]did, [8]got, [9]was thinking, [10]remembered, [11]thought, [12]went, [13]did he do, [14]saw, [15]wanted, [16]travelled, [17]arrived, [18]was stepping/stepped, [19]started, [20]turned, [21]was only wearing, [22]soon had, [23]didn't mind, [24]went, [25]drove, [26]bought, [27]needed, [28]didn't have to, [29]took, [30]was, [31]told, [32]rang, [33]was he doing, [34]was still lying, [35](was) sleeping, [36]thought, [37]was

ufgabe 8

a) Did you drop the picture when you were tidying your room?
b) What were they doing at five o'clock yesterday when their aunt arrived?
c) Were your parents sleeping when you came back from the party?
d) Who was reading the news when she turned on the TV?
e) Did you meet her when you were going to the cinema?
f) Was your mother working in the garden when I rang you up?
g) Did John visit the castles on his way when he was driving to his aunt's?
h) Did they hear the loud noise when they were playing in the garden?

Aufgabe 9

Our holiday this year was terrible. The years before, we usually had to go with our parents, but this year we were allowed to go by train alone. When we were sitting in the train, the guard/ticket collector came and wanted to see our tickets. When my brother Jeff couldn't find them at once/immediately, the guard wanted to throw us off the train at the next station. But luckily, I found the tickets in the pocket of my trousers. At the bed and breakfast (place) we had difficulties, too: the landlady wanted to give us a small room. We were still talking to her, when another man said behind us, "Children ought to stay/sleep at the youth hostel!" But at last/finally/eventually we were able to convince/persuade her and she gave us the key to our room. Five minutes later, we were already unpacking our suitcases. That wasn't all: so many terrible things happened on that holiday that we left the bed and breakfast (place) earlier than (we had) planned and went back home (again) as fast as possible.

Aufgabe 10
a) She has arrived at her hotel
b) She has unpacked her suitcase.
c) She hasn't put her shoes in the wardrobe.
d) She has bought a postcard.
e) She hasn't eaten all her biscuits.
f) She has started to read a book.

Aufgabe 11
a) They've gone to Italy on holiday.
b) Sorry, I've forgotten my book.
c) Where have you put my watch?
d) Has anybody come?
e) I haven't tasted this lemonade.
f) Where have you gone?
g) I haven't seen "Cats" yet.
h) The passengers have gone.
i) I'm afraid I've lost my money.
j) I've checked your tyres.
k) You haven't sent us a reservation.

Aufgabe 12
a) has been painting
b) has been eating
c) has been digging
d) have been driving
e) have been playing
f) has been running

Aufgabe 13
a) has been reading, for
b) have been sitting, since

c) have been cleaning
d) Have you been washing, for
e) haven't been playing, have been talking
f) has been swimming, since
g) have they been doing
h) Haven't you been tidying, since
i) has been raining, for

fgabe 14 Mrs Baker has been looking at all the sights for an hour and a half.
I have been going to this school all my life.
You have never had to be alone for so long.
He has been working at this factory these past few years.
She has been listening to records since two o'clock.
This garden has belonged to us for years.
We have lived in London since you last saw me.
They have been in the house for twenty minutes.
My parents have been driving our car all day.
The Greens have seen Tower Bridge three times since yesterday.

ufgabe 15 [1]have been cleaning, [2]have fed, [3]have hung, [4]have left, [5]has carried, [6]have washed, [7]haven't put, [8]haven't made, [9]have been working, [10]Have you seen, [11]has taken, [12]have been looking, [13]have found, [14]haven't had, [15]have you been doing, [16]haven't been sleeping

ufgabe 16 Last year, Mrs Kent, our butcher's wife, went on holiday alone because her husband didn't want to close down/shut the shop. She said: "I (have) found such a cheap offer for a flight to California in the newspaper! We have never been to California and all our customers say that that's the cheapest trip to America there has been for years!" So Mr Kent let her go, although he didn't like staying at home. Before she set off, she had to go to the bank and change some money. When the bank clerk wanted to give her her dollar bills, another customer started to talk/talking. He said: "I've always found it great when I was in America. I know what I'm talking about: I've already spent my holidays there eight times, and I've just come back/returned from New York again." "Really?/Have you?" Mrs Kent asked him. "Then you must tell me everything about the country and the people! Have the people always been friendly to you? Have you ever had any problems with the police? What sights have you already seen/visited? Did you have a good flight? Who helped you when you were in trouble/difficulties? Which towns did you like best? …"

Aufgabe 17

a) … had taken … tried to get …
b) … had tried … visited …
c) … she had visited one of the …, she took a walk through …
d) When she had taken a walk through Central Park, she rode one of the yellow taxis.
e) After she had ridden one of the yellow taxis, she looked down from the Statue of Liberty.
f) After she had looked down from the Statue of Liberty, she went to the outskirts by subway.

Aufgabe 18

a) Because I had heard so many terrible stories about the city.
b) Because I had read a lot of beautiful books about the USA.
c) Because they had written me a letter saying they would be on holiday at that time.
d) Because my cousin had told me a lot about New York.
e) Because I hadn't tried to get a ticket early enough.
f) Because I hadn't thought New York was so great.
g) Because I hadn't liked the flight to the USA.
h) Because I hadn't been in the USA before.
i) Because I hadn't asked my parents early enough.
j) Because I hadn't thought of that possibility.
k) Because everybody had asked me for presents from the USA.

Aufgabe 19

a) had been playing, for
b) had been talking, since
c) had been washing, for
d) had been cleaning, for
e) had been flying, since
f) had been standing, for

gabe 20
a) ... had been cleaning his room before the telephone rang.
b) ... had been sitting in the bathtub/having a bath before the telephone rang.
c) ... had been working in the garden before the telephone rang.
d) ... had been playing a game before the telephone rang.
e) ... had been lying in bed before the telephone rang.
f) ... had been watching TV before the telephone rang.
g) ... had been going upstairs before the telephone rang.

gabe 21*
a) We had been looking down from the Empire State Building for an hour when we met Aunt Evelyn.
b) She had lived in Detroit for ten years, since the beginning of her studies at university when she moved to Cincinnati.
c) They had been walking through Central Park from six to eight, when they took a taxi to their hotel.
d) I had known that theatre for years when I saw it yesterday for the first time since its renovation.
e) After my brother had been reading a book since breakfast, we had pizza for lunch.
f) Had you been on holiday until you came back home last week?
g) When the performance began at half past eight, I had been waiting for my friend for an hour.
h) After he had bought a new suit, he drove to California last week.
i) Patty had been preparing sandwiches for two hours when she started making tea.
j) She looked nice again after she had gone to the hairdresser's yesterday.
k) When Mike rang up his mother at twelve, he had been cooking for one hour.

fgabe 22*
[1]has, [2]had, [3]have, [4]have, [5]had, [6]had, [7]has, [8]has, [9]have, [10]had, [11]had, [12]have

Aufgabe 23* [1]did you spend, [2]had spent, [3]stayed, [4]for, [5]hadn't been, [6]for, [7]hadn't you told/didn't you tell, [8]left, [9]had originally booked, [10]had come, [11]told, [12]could, [13]was, [14]have never seen, [15]have spoken, [16]became, [17]were talking, [18]have been describing, [19]for, [20]have been talking, [21]since, [22]came, [23]did you come, [24]have been working, [25]for, [26]was, [27]weren't you/hadn't you been, [28]had never flown, [29]had, [30]had been trembling, [31]for, [32]took, [33]really liked, [34]were flying, [35]served, [36]also got, [37]wasn't, [38]was taking off, [39]started, [40]wanted, [41]was going, [42]calmed, [43]haven't heard, [44]have you been doing, [45]since, [46]saw, [47]bought, [48]delivered, [49]had really been looking, [50]for, [51]haven't had, [52]absolutely had to, [53]have been repairing, [54]cleaning, [55]haven't taken, [56]for

Aufgabe 24

a) "Have you been to the top of the Statue of Liberty yet?"

b) "Did you go and see 'The Lion King' this week?"

c) "Who had booked the tickets for you?"

d) "What were you doing when I started talking to you?"

e) "What had you been listening to before the trip started?"

f) "Since when has this woman been reading?"

g) "Have you had lunch yet?"

h) "Why haven't you had lunch yet?"

i) "Did you go to the movies last week?"

j) "Where did you have to go?"

Aufgabe 25 Have you ever been to New York? I visited the city last year with a few friends of mine, and I liked it very much. I had never seen such a big city before. After we had unpacked our suitcases, we went for a walk in Central Park, because we were too tired to go on a big sightseeing tour. Over the next few days/During the following days we then visited everything our friends and relatives had been talking about for years. But the terrible air kept bothering us. In Ireland, where we had spent our holidays in a small village the year before, the air is much better. And there are a lot of/many animals there, not only/just cars. Nevertheless we were able to/could understand that the New Yorkers like living/to live in their city, because we had a lot of/many nice experiences/adventures (which/that) we certainly won't forget.

gabe 26* [1]was, [2]fall, [3]was standing, [4]sidewalk, [5]skyscraper, [6]crossing, [7]was, [8]subway, [9]heard, [10]sixth floor, [11]was, [12]had thought, [13]was, [14]movies, [15]didn't/couldn't understand, [16]was saying, [17]truck, [18]was driving, [19]made, [20]had already disappeared, [21]went, [22]had parked, [23]parking lot, [24]gas station, [25]met, [26]students, [27]principal, [28]were working, [29]trailer, [30]had never seen, [31]asked, [32]have you been working, [33]answered,[34] apartment, [35]did

The two words which are written differently in AE are: centre – center, colours – colors

Zeiten der Zukunft

ufgabe 1

a) You will be rich. / You'll be rich.
b) You will live for a long time.
c) You will move to the USA.
d) You will have a lot of children.
e) You will get a nice job.

ufgabe 2

a) Will there be as many wars in the future as (there were) in the past?
b) When will people finally learn that they live better in peace?
c) What will have to happen so that everybody believes it at last?
d) Without war everyone will at last sleep quietly/in peace.

ufgabe 3

a) On Monday, he's going to play tennis.
b) On Tuesday, he's going to have a picnic.
c) On Wednesday, he's going to visit a museum.
d) On Thursday, Tom and Priscilla are going to go swimming.
e) On Friday, they are going to go shopping.
f) On Saturday, Tom is going to fly his model plane.
g) On Sunday, he is going to stay in bed all day.

Aufgabe 4

a) TOM: Are you going to play tennis with me tomorrow?
PATRICIA: No, I'm going to work in my uncle's shop.

b) TOM: Are you going to have a picnic with me on Tuesday/the day after tomorrow?
PATRICIA: No, I'm going to visit my cousins.

c) TOM: Are you going to visit a museum with me on Wednesday?
PATRICIA: No, I'm going to play with my baby sister.

d) TOM: Are you going to go swimming with Priscilla and me on Thursday?
PATRICIA: No, I'm going to play volleyball.

e) TOM: Are you going to go shopping with us on Friday?
PATRICIA: No, I'm going to do some work for school.

f) TOM: Are you going to fly your model plane on Saturday, too?
PATRICIA: No, I'm going to go on a bicycle tour.

g) TOM: Are you going to stay in bed all Sunday, too?
PATRICIA: No, I'm going to watch TV.

Aufgabe 5

[1]are your parents coming/going to come, [2]will/are going to be, [3]is, [4]will have to, [5]Are you going to go, [6]will/am going to clean/am cleaning/will be cleaning, [7]starts, [8]am going to work, [9]are you going to do, [10]am going to learn/am learning, [11]won't do

Aufgabe 6

aren't, staying, am going, will meet/am meeting; does/will, leave, leaves; are going to visit/are visiting

Aufgabe 7*

I don't think that the future will be like in all those science fiction films. *einleitende Meinungsäußerung*

First of all, I don't believe there are living beings on other planets. And even if there were any, I am sure we wouldn't be able to communicate with them as easily as the film characters do. *Begründung I*

In addition, I really doubt that technical progress will ever make it possible for human beings to fly into space at speeds and at distances as they show them in the films. *Begründung II*

Finally, I hope one aspect of the future will be really different: most science fiction films show a lot of warfare, and I hope for a future of peace on earth. Begründung III

So, all in all, science fiction films are simply very unrealistic; the real future will certainly be different. zusammenfassende Schlussbemerkung

Konditional und Bedingungssätze

Aufgabe 1

a) I would buy a big house.
b) I would travel round the world.
c) I would give the money to my grandchildren.
d) I would never go to work again.
e) We would travel to New York.
f) I would drive an expensive car.
g) I would eat French fries every day.
h) We would open a shop.

Aufgabe 2

a) I would have gone swimming.
b) I would have flown my kite.
c) I would have gone for a walk in the park.
d) I would have ridden my bike.
e) I would have played with my friends.
f) I would have washed my parents' car.

Aufgabe 3

a) They would have bought a big house.
b) They would have travelled round the world.
c) They would have given the money to their grandchildren.
d) They would never have gone to work again.
e) They wouldn't have travelled to New York.
f) They wouldn't have driven/bought an expensive car.
g) They wouldn't have eaten French fries every day.
h) They wouldn't have opened a shop.

Aufgabe 4*

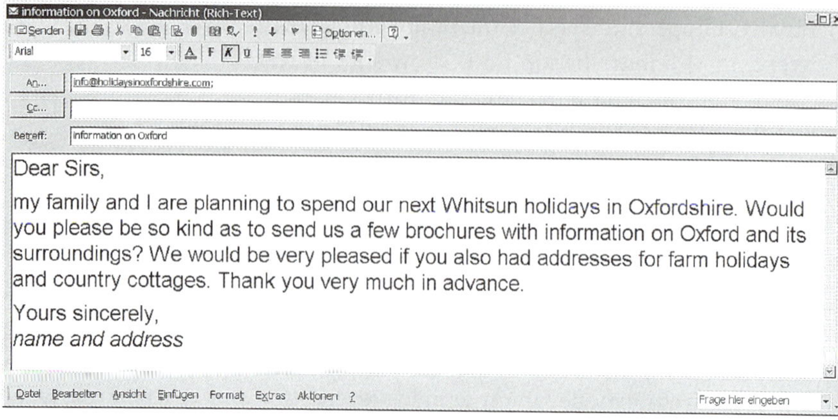

information on Oxford - Nachricht (Rich-Text)

An... info@holidaysinoxfordshire.com;

Cc...

Betreff: information on Oxford

Dear Sirs,

my family and I are planning to spend our next Whitsun holidays in Oxfordshire. Would you please be so kind as to send us a few brochures with information on Oxford and its surroundings? We would be very pleased if you also had addresses for farm holidays and country cottages. Thank you very much in advance.

Yours sincerely,
name and address

Aufgabe 5

a) will stay
b) will
c) come early, will
d) play longer, will
e) is much nicer, will
f) am happier, will
g) don't quarrel so much, will
h) let me go to the cinema, will
i) see that great film at last, will be able

Aufgabe 6

a) If there were no school today, I would stay at home all day.
b) If I stayed at home all day, my friends would come early.
c) If my friends came early, we would play longer than usual.
d) If we played longer than usual, the day would be much nicer.
e) If the day were nicer, I would be happier.
f) If I were happier, my parents and I wouldn't quarrel so much.
g) If we didn't quarrel so much, they would let me go to the cinema.
h) If they let me go to the cinema, I would at last see that great film.
i) If I saw that great film at last, I would be able to talk about it with my classmates.

Aufgabe 7

a) If there had been no school yesterday, I would have stayed at home all day.
b) If I had stayed at home all day, my friends would have come early.
c) If my friends had come early, we would have played longer than usual.

d) If we had played longer than usual, the day would have been much nicer.

e) If the day had been nicer, I would have been happier.

f) If I had been happier, my parents and I wouldn't have quarreled so much.

g) If we hadn't quarreled so much, they would have let me go to the cinema.

h) If they had let me go to the cinema, I would at last have seen that great film.

i) If I had seen that great film at last, I would have been able to talk about it with my classmates.

ufgabe 8 [1]won't go, [2]had known, [3]watch, [4]would go, [5]were, [6]would know, [7]would have been, [8]will have to

ufgabe 9 [1]will/would laugh, [2]wear/wore, [3]don't like, [4]will like, [5]is, [6]will have to, [7]were, [8]would buy, [9]had told, [10]wouldn't have shown, [11]hadn't seen, [12]wouldn't have come, [13]don't find, [14]will go, [15]had thought, [16]would have found, [17]isn't, [18]will leave, [19]won't, [20]had, [21]would certainly show, [22]will have to, [23]want

gabe 10* a 4: If Thomas Alva Edison hadn't invented the light bulb, we would have to go to bed much earlier.

b 8: If John D. Rockefeller hadn't made so much money, the Rockefeller Foundation wouldn't have been able to help so many gifted people since it was founded.

c 2: If the Wright Brothers had given up after their first attempts, perhaps modern planes wouldn't exist.

d 1: If we had no electricity, all the inventors' efforts would have been in vain.

e 3: If he hadn't known that he would make a lot of money with it, Elias Howe would not have tried to invent a sewing-machine.

f 6: If life today is much easier than life in the past, it is certainly because of all the good ideas some people have had.

g 7: If printers hadn't started to introduce typewriters in the 1880s, the development of computers would not have become possible.

h 5: If Henry Ford hadn't produced his Model T on the assembly line, he wouldn't have sold thousands of cars in a few months.

Aufgabe 11*

a) If people hadn't had $ 24 to buy the island from the Indians, New York couldn't have been built as it was.

b) If Manhattan weren't so big, you could walk from its northern end to its southern end.

c) If the skyscrapers weren't so high, you could see the sun in every street.

d) If the Empire State Building weren't higher than the Chrysler Building, it wouldn't be the highest skyscraper in Manhattan.

e) If an architect finds space in Manhattan, he will build a house in it.

f) If there were more space, architects who want to build new skyscrapers wouldn't be ready to tear down old ones.

g) Today Manhattan wouldn't be so famous if it didn't have/weren't for its skyline.

h) The streets in Manhattan wouldn't have been laid out like a chess board if one mayor hadn't decided this would make the island more attractive.

i) If Central Park didn't exist, the inhabitants of Manhattan couldn't breathe fresh air.

Aufgabe 12

a) If Robin Hood and his men hadn't always been disguised/in disguise, the Sheriff of Nottingham would have recognized them at once/ immediately.

b) When their clothes were old and torn, they went to Lincoln Market.

c) Robin always said/used to say: "If you find something else, you can buy that, too."

d) Often his men answered/replied: "Okay, if we see something else, we'll buy it.

e) But if we had more money, we would be able to/could buy even more.

f) We would have more money, if you had allowed us to/had let us rob even more rich people."

g) "I don't think so," Robin used to answer/reply, "because if we had more money, you would long have spent it.

h) You know, when you see something nice, you always want to have it at once/immediately.

i) And then/By the way/Besides you mustn't forget: if we robbed the rich (in order) to use the money for ourselves, we wouldn't be outlaws but plain/ordinary thieves."

Passiv

fgabe 1

a) The tank is filled up.
b) The wheel is changed.
c) The hubcap is put on again/ back on.
d) The oil is checked.
e) Cars are washed.
f) The horn of a car is repaired.
g) The battery of an old Rolls Royce is looked at.
h) A lot of things are sold.

ufgabe 2

a) was dropped
b) were thrown
c) was felled
d) was lifted
e) was mowed
f) was closed

ufgabe 3

a) When I arrived at the filling station, the tank of my car was just being filled up.
b) When I arrived at the filling station, a wheel of my car was just being changed.
c) When I arrived at the filling station, the hubcap was just being put on again/back on.
d) When I arrived at the filling station, the oil was just being checked.
e) When I arrived at the filling station, a few cars were just being washed.
f) When I arrived at the filling station, the horn of a car was just being repaired.
g) When I arrived at the filling station, the battery of an old Rolls Royce was just being looked at.
h) When I arrived at the filling station, a lot of things were just being sold.

Aufgabe 4

a) The river has been polluted for days.
b) It had to be cleaned.
c) Everybody hopes that the police will be informed.

d) The criminal is just being looked for.

e) He hasn't been found yet.

f) Nobody knows if he will really be caught.

Aufgabe 5

a) Cars and the environment

b) Driving a car is bad for the environment, but something can be done to limit the destruction.

Only few car drivers are aware of the negative effects their cars have on the environment. But everybody should know by now that the noise they produce makes people ill, that streets and roads destroy nature and that the exhaust fumes cause the greenhouse effect. But we can reduce these damages. If cars need less petrol, and if that petrol is less toxic, and if people use their cars more consciously, the exhaust fumes will be dramatically reduced. Better public transportation systems would be helpful, too, because car drivers would use them more often instead of going by car.

c) An environment-conscious car driver should buy a silent car that needs little petrol, even if this means that he cannot accelerate or drive as quickly as with another car.

d) There are three main negative effects of car driving on the environment. Firstly, cars make a lot of noise, and noise can make people ill. Secondly, when new roads and motorways are built, trees must be felled and fields are destroyed, and the living space for many animals is reduced. Thirdly, the exhaust fumes of cars are responsible for the greenhouse effect, which is changing the climate in many parts of the world.

e) Both catalytic converters and less gas-guzzling cars would help to reduce the amount of poisonous substances in the exhaust fumes of cars, and with it the destruction of the environment.

f) Firstly, people will have to be ready to pay more for driving their cars. The technology needed to produce less gas-guzzling cars is expensive, as is research for better petrol. Secondly, car drivers will have to change their customs and go by public transport (or by bike or on foot) more often, especially when they don't go far.

g)
- "When asked about their cars, …"
  When somebody asks them about their cars, …
- "Cars are still widely seen …"
  People still widely see their cars …

- "... your friends and neighbours will be impressed."
  ... you will impress your friends and neighbours.
- "... which have to be built ..."
  ... which the state has to build ...
- "... technical progress is needed."
  ... we need technical progress.
- "... public transport must be made even more attractive, ..."
  ... the state/we/the government must make public transport even more attractive, ...
- "... and be driven to their destination ..."
  ... and to let buses drive them to their destination

fgabe 6 No thought is given by many car drivers to the pollution which might be caused by the burning of their cars' fuel. In addition, every minute, tons of dirt are being let into the rivers and a lot of smoke into the air by factories. The air or the water might be polluted by most of the things which are produced (by man) and which are needed in everyday life. The traces which are left by cars, central heating and plastic bags can be found everywhere. On the other hand, a lot can be read and heard about pollution and its effects. It is known today that new ideas are needed. But are better systems already being produced? Is the pollution of the seas, lakes and rivers being fought? New ideas must be developed if man doesn't want the world to be completely destroyed. One example are new plastic bags: they can easily be burnt/, which are easily burnt. If nature isn't helped by man, it is certain to die.

fgabe 7* [1]be left, [2]was raised, [3]is given/has been given, [4]has been/is recognised, [5]is practised, [6]will be recycled, [7]be made, [8]be thrown, [9]have been put up, [10]is collected

ufgabe 8
a) Nature is not always taken care of.
b) Environmental problems cannot be easily coped with.
c) New ideas are constantly being talked about.
d) Warners are sometimes/have sometimes been laughed at.
e) Environmentalists are not always listened to.

Aufgabe 9

a) Somebody has written Linda a letter.
A letter has been written to Linda.
Linda has been written a letter.

b) Somebody has handed Rosie a newspaper.
A newspaper has been handed to Rosie.
Rosie has been handed a newspaper.

c) Somebody has sold the Clarks a house.
A house has been sold to the Clarks.
The Clarks have been sold a house.

d) Somebody has given Billy some extra homework.
Some extra homework has been given to Billy.
Billy has been given some extra homework.

e) Somebody has offered Mr Riley a cheap car.
A cheap car has been offered to Mr Riley.
Mr Riley has been offered a cheap car.

f) Somebody has taught Milly a song.
A song has been taught to Milly.
Milly has been taught a song.

Aufgabe 10

[1]have been felled, [2]were built, [3]hasn't been changed, [4]was made, [5]is done

Aufgabe 11*

When people were driving the first cars through the London streets, Parliament made a law saying that a man with a red flag had to warn pedestrians and horse coaches. In some American towns, the city government fixed the speed limit at 10 miles per hour. New York was the first city to offer its policemen bicycles so that they could catch cars driving too fast. Today, we can only laugh at such stories. And in future? Will something new replace cars? And how much will people fear this new thing in the beginning?

Aufgabe 12*

a) Cooper gave Natty Bumppo the name Leatherstocking.
Natty Bumppo was given the name Leatherstocking (by Cooper).

b) He wrote his novels in the 1820's, 1830's and 1840's.
The "Leatherstocking" novels were written in the 1820's, 1830's and 1840's.

c) Cooper based Leatherstocking on the model of Daniel Boone.
Leatherstocking was based on the model of Daniel Boone.

d) Civilization fought the wilderness.
The wilderness was fought by civilization.

e) The settlers destroyed the beauty and liberty of the woods.
The beauty and liberty of the woods were destroyed by the settlers.

f) He shot a deer out of season.
A deer was shot by him out of season.

g) The townsmen fired into flocks of passenger pigeons.
Flocks of passenger pigeons were fired into.

gabe 13* The scene of this painting is set in wooded mountains, with one high peak in the background and a big lake in the foreground, and without any trace of civilization nearby. It probably is a picture from the early days of the American pioneers. There are several boats or canoes on the lake. The people in them – maybe Indians – do not seem to be fishing, they might just be taking a pleasure ride. The scene is very peaceful, it looks as if nothing could disturb the silence of this moment out in the wilderness.
title: Out on the lake

Infinitiv

ufgabe 1 [1]to sweep, [2]to water, [3]to hang, [4]to watch, [5]to pull, [6]to serve, [7]to paint, [8]to transport, [9]to dig, [10]to cut, [11]to make, [12]to be

ufgabe 2

a) how to prepare
b) what to say
c) how to look for
d) what to do
e) who to ask
f) what, to choose
g) whether to travel
h) how to make
i) how to get up
j) where to go

ufgabe 3

a) It wasn't easy for the settlers to get in contact with Indians.
b) There were lots of opportunities for them to meet some of them.

c) But most settlers thought it was too dangerous for them to go and talk with Indians.
d) Of course the Indians didn't want the whites to be on their land.
e) In the end there were too many whites for the Indians to be able to beat them.
f) Sometimes they waited for Indian tribes to fight against each other.
g) Some whites would have preferred the Indians to die.
h) It was easy for them to kill Indians because they had guns.

Aufgabe 4
a) ... the peace.
b) ... you not to make any unnecessary noise.
c) ... for you not to litter the streets.
d) ... you to feed your animals well.
e) ... you to drink or gamble.
f) ... for everybody to go to church regularly.
g) ... to be friendly to your neighbors.
h) ... for us/anybody to help you if you attack anybody without reason.

Aufgabe 5
a) The settlers came to the wild west (in order) to start a new life.
b) The towns on the east coast were too crowded to offer them work/a job and a place to live.
c) All the problems in the towns made them look for something new and many thought, "We will be able to live better elsewhere/somewhere else."
d) None of them spoke/was able to speak one of the Indians' languages and they only sometimes found somebody to help them.
e) This is why they often did not know what to do when they met Indians.
f) "The best thing to do is smile," they had been told.

Aufgabe 6
[1]tell, [2]go, [3]follow, [4]try, [5]manage, [6]repair, [7]sit, [8]do

fgabe 7

a) What names of famous Indians can you remember?
b) Probably you have already heard someone mention the name of Sitting bull.
c) Sitting Bull was one of the first Indians to become world-famous.
d) The Sioux believed that it would be possible for him to lead and protect them.
e) So they wanted him to be their leader when he was still very young.
f) In the Battle of the Rosebud, Sitting Bull and his warriors made the government troops retreat.
g) Nine days later, on June 25, 1876, at the little Big Horn, it soon became clear that it would be impossible for General Custer to defeat Sitting Bull.
h) Later in his life, the whites made Sitting Bull live on Standing Rock Reservation.
i) He died in a struggle with the Indian police who didn't let him leave the reservation, following an invitation to Pine Ridge Reservation.

Gerundium

ufgabe 1

a) Throwing
b) Knocking
c) Cutting
d) meeting/seeing, quarrelling
e) looking
f) Breaking
g) getting up

ufgabe 2

[1]travelling, [2]finding, [3]staying, [4]living, [5]staying, [6]spending, [7]repairing, [8]caring, [9]working, [10]cooking, [11]looking, [12]having, [13]meeting, [14]staying, [15]being

ufgabe 3

a) The whites took all the land away from the Indians without asking anybody.
b) Before taking the land, they killed nearly all the buffalo.
c) The Indians needed the buffalo for surviving.
d) After eating their meat, they also made tents out of their skins.
e) But instead of eating all the meat, the whites left the dead buffalo lying on the prairies.
f) The whites used the buffalo for having fun.

g) But many whites killed the buffalo without thinking of the fact that this would be dangerous for the Indians.

h) Very soon, the Indians realised that the whites would kill them by killing the buffalo.

i) And that is what really happened. After nearly destroying all the buffalo, the whites nearly destroyed the Indians.

Aufgabe 4

a) expecting/having expected an easier life, first coming to the west

b) of the Indians/Indians' being a danger, about not being disturbed, building up their farm

c) coming/having come to the west, to the climate being different from that in the east

d) of being able to do a lot with wood, of having built the whole house alone

e) of his family/his family's leaving the farm again

f) about having survived, his family/his family's nearly dying

good order of the sentences: c – b – d – f – e – a

Aufgabe 5*

Not all new settlers succeeded in living a better life in the west. Many of them kept saying that they preferred living in the east. "How/What about going back where we came from?", many women asked their husbands, although they had decided on going west together.
But the men only answered, "It's no use going back. Stop telling me we should leave the west." "But we had no idea about keeping a farm before arriving here, and now we see that we have a lot of difficulty in farming. I can't help thinking about how nice life would be elsewhere." "Rubbish! We'll stay here! I think it's worth staying here. And then, stop worrying and rather go and work, so our chance of having a good harvest this year will be better/so we will have a better chance of having a good harvest this year!"

Aufgabe 6

a) shouting/being angry, on seeing, buying/booking

b) fishing, sitting, to spending, of looking at/watching, catching, talking about/discussing, fishing

c) in walking, walking, climbing, looking, of getting/feeling, smiling fgabe 7 [1]to speak, [2]to be inhabited, [3]living, [4]in creating, [5]to separate, [6]to practise, [7]to come, [8]to arrive, [9]to survive, [10]in surviving, [11]living, [12]at hearing/to hear, [13]to explain, [14]to stay, [15]to return, [16]to finally make, [17]about being/to be, [18]to fish, [19]acting/to act, [20]of being, [21]to plant, [22]planting, [23]to make, [24]to help/helping, [25]get, [26]helping, [27]on giving/to give, [27]by burying

ıfgabe 8 avoided telling
were busy telling
couldn't tell
dare tell
expected me to tell
forgot to tell
gave up telling
were happy about telling/to tell
imagine telling
justified in telling
keen on telling
let me tell
made me tell
no good telling
ordered them to tell
preferred telling/to tell
qualified to tell
remembered telling/to tell
stopped telling/to tell
were told to tell
unusual for them to tell
vicious enough to tell
when telling
too young to tell
zealous to tell
Perhaps they had got good marks at school?

Aufgabe 9 Before landing in America, Columbus was at sea for months. He and his men had difficulty in surviving and in his diary he kept complaining about having to drink bad water. But the Spanish king had promised to make them rich, and so they didn't stop hoping for better times; after all, the king expected them to finish their voyage. The sailors relied on their captain's hopes(') being founded. Later Columbus remembered seeing land at last. It was difficult for him to believe that he had really succeeded in putting his plan into action.

Partizip

Aufgabe 1

a) JENNY: ... flowers
FATHER: ... gardener

b) JENNY: This is a woman typing letters.
FATHER: I see. This is a secretary.

c) JENNY: This is a woman teaching children/pupils.
FATHER: I see. This is a teacher.

d) JENNY: This is a woman driving a racing-car.
FATHER: I see. This is a racing-driver.

e) JENNY: This is a woman selling clothes.
FATHER: I see. This is a shop assistant.

f) JENNY: This is a woman making shoes.
FATHER: I see. This is a shoemaker.

Aufgabe 2

a) ... the gardener.

b) These are the letters typed by the secretary.

c) These are the pupils/children/schoolchildren taught by the teacher.

d) This is the racing-car driven by the racing-driver.

e) These are the clothes sold by the shop assistant.

f) These are the shoes made by the shoemaker.

Aufgabe 3

Wanting to buy herself a motor-bike, Amy does everything this year to find a good holiday job. Still, she doesn't want to take the one offered her by her uncle in his grocer's shop: working eight hours a day, she wants to earn more than £ 100 a week! (While) Reading the newspaper one morning, she suddenly sees an advert saying: "Are you one of those youngsters looking for a job? You don't like any of the jobs advertised for in the papers? And you don't like jobs getting you only little money? Then come and see us immediately! (Being) Paid extremely well, the workers at our petrol station are really happy!"

Going there, Amy got a job. She made a lot of money (by) washing cars, checking the oil and cleaning windscreens. And after the holidays, being very proud, she said to her uncle: "I will never work for somebody paying his workers as badly as you do!"

ufgabe 4 (When) Dreaming of a great job, many youngsters/young people think of becoming flight attendants. They have heard that it's a lot of fun flying from one country to another. But they forget that it's also hard work serving the passengers food and drinks for hours. Furthermore/In addition, only the flight attendants employed by/working for big airlines earn a lot. (Being) Disappointed with/by their job, after a few years many flight attendants look for another job offering them more. It is also important to know that the airlines only take/employ well-trained/well-educated young women and men speaking foreign languages.

ufgabe 5

a) People leading the way are called pioneers. / We call people leading the way pioneers.
b) Yes, the first American colonists coming to the east were pioneers.
c) They settled along the Atlantic Coast, changing the forest area into a land of towns and farms.
d) Across the mountains lay/was another forest, then called the American Frontier.
e) The mountains separating this forest from the thirteen colonies being steep and difficult to cross, the pioneers stayed at the coast for a long time.
f) Indians living in the area west of the mountains were unfriendly, saying they would always keep the white men out.
g) No, it didn't. A few brave hunters fought the Indians crossing the mountains.
h) Daniel Boone was one of the pioneers leading the way.
i) John Findlay was a scout and Indian fighter; having been to the west of the mountains he had returned with stories of the beautiful land called Kentucky by the Indians. / … fighter who had been to the west of the mountains, returning with stories …
j) Talking a lot about Kentucky to Boone, John Findlay filled Daniel's head with the idea of moving there.

k) No, they didn't. Boone organized a wagon trail to the land of his dreams, leading his own family and other families to Kentucky.

l) In 1775, Daniel Boone, his family and some of his friends started a settlement called Boonesborough.

m) Started by Boone, his family and his friends, Boonesborough grew fast.

n) Boone's efforts, planned for a long time, opened the way to the west, an adventure beginning the growth of the United States in this direction.

Aufgabe 6
a) ... his hair cut.
b) ... makes his apprentice clean/sweep the floor.
c) ... lets her workers go home.
d) ... has her watch repaired.
e) ... are made to work faster.
f) ... let the child pick the flowers.

Relativsätze

Aufgabe 1
a) ... the car which Henry Ford made. (3)
b) ... is the man who invented the telephone. (6)
c) Neil Armstrong was the first man who landed/walked on the moon. (2)
d) ... is the man who invented the light bulb. (4)
e) The American Red Cross is the organization whose founder was ... (1)
f) Abraham Lincoln is the man who was killed by John Wilkes Booth. / Abraham Lincoln is the man whose murderer was John Wilkes Booth. (5)

Aufgabe 2
a) Charles Lindbergh, man that flew
b) Florence Nightingale, men that were wounded
c) Thomas Jefferson, –
d) Queen Elizabeth II, –
e) Ulysses Simpson Grant, town that was captured
f) Charles Goodyear, discovery that made
g) Ella Fitzgerald, name that was given
h) Horatio Nelson, battle that this man won, but that he was also killed in

fgabe 3 [1]which/that, [2]who/that, [3]whose, [4]who, [5]who(m), [6]whose, [7]which, [8]which/that, [9]which/that, [10]who/that, [11]who

fgabe 4 [1]that; [2]who; [3]who/that; [4]which/that; [5], whose; [6]which/that; France,; [7]whose; [8](which/that); [9], on which; [10](which/that); [11]whose; [12]which/that; [13](which/that); [14](who/whom/that); [15], who; life,; [16]whom

fgabe 5
a) ... Rockefeller built a skyscraper in. / ... in which Rockefeller built a skyscraper.
b) ... the country Europeans have always dreamed of. / ... the country of which Europeans have always dreamed.
c) The USA is the country a lot of inventors came from. / The USA is the country from which a lot of inventors came.
d) Virginia is the American state Thomas Jefferson was born in. / Virginia is the American state in which Thomas Jefferson was born.
e) Gettysburg is the town Lincoln delivered a famous speech in. / Gettysburg is the town in which Lincoln delivered a famous speech.
f) The Appalachians are the mountains frontiersmen like Daniel Boone led the early settlers through. / The Appalachians are the mountains through which frontiersmen like Daniel Boone led the early settlers.
g) Washington is the city Martin Luther King went to for his speech 'I have a dream'. / Washington is the city to which Martin Luther King went for his speech 'I have a dream'.
h) Dallas is the city John F. Kennedy was killed in. / Dallas is the city in which John F. Kennedy was killed.

ufgabe 6
a) The adventure Lindbergh succeeded in was to fly from the USA to Europe alone. (in which Lindbergh succeeded)
b) The name Florence Nightingale was called by was "the lady with the lamp". / "The lady with the lamp" was the name Florence Nightingale was called by. (by which Florence Nightingale was called)
c) The piece of writing Thomas Jefferson became famous for was the Declaration of Independence. / The Declaration of Independence was the piece

of writing Thomas Jefferson became famous for. (for which Thomas Jefferson became famous)

d) The woman I look at is Queen Elizabeth II. / Queen Elizabeth II is the woman I look at in the fourth picture. (whom/ who I look at)

e) The man Vicksburg was captured by was Ulysses Simpson Grant. / Ulysses Simpson Grant was the man Vicksburg was captured by. (by whom/who Vicksburg was captured)

f) Tyres are the product rubber is ideal for. / The product rubber is ideal for are tyres. (for which rubber is ideal)

g) The name Ella Fitzgerald was known by was "First Lady of Jazz". / "First Lady of Jazz" was the name Ella Fitzgerald was known by. (by which Ella Fitzgerald was known)

h) The battle Horatio Nelson was killed in took place at Trafalgar. (in which Horatio Nelson was killed)

Aufgabe 7 Horatio Nelson, whose parents sent him to school in Norfolk, joined the navy in 1770, at the age of 12. His mother's brother, who was a navy captain himself, helped him. The only problem he wasn't able to/couldn't solve throughout his whole life was his seasickness, for which he was smiled at by many: Nelson, who was to become Great Britain's greatest naval officer, constantly fought against nausea/being sick! The battle Nelson finally became famous for took place in 1805. The ship he sailed into the Battle of Trafalgar on was called "Victory". He defeated France and Spain, who had sent 33 ships. England was saved from Napoleon, who now had to stay on the European continent.

Aufgabe 8 a) After the American Revolution, the country, which had been a small territory along the Atlantic coast before, grew, and its western frontier was the Mississippi.

b) The second great step was the Louisiana Purchase, with which the size of the country was suddenly increased by one third.

c) The treaty was not clear on the exact western limits of the new territory, which were not known.

d) The important fact was that no strong foreign power held territory to the west of the young United States, who/which was free to grow in the direction of the Pacific.

e) There was little interest in the Louisiana territory, which was bought in 1803. / The Louisiana territory, which there was little interest in/ in which there was little interest, was bought in 1803.

f) The land, which was unknown to most Americans, seemed very far away to them. / The land, which seemed very far away to most Americans, was unknown to them. / The land was unknown to most Americans, to who(m) it seemed very far away. / The land seemed very far away to most Americans, to who(m) it was unknown.

g) But the Mississippi was of importance to many of the settlers of Kentucky and Tennessee, who had no other way of selling their farm products but to ship them down the Mississippi to New Orleans.

h) But many times the port of New Orleans was closed to American shipping by Spanish officials there, who were often changed by the government in Spain; others suddenly closed the port without explanation.

i) President Jefferson was also worried about Napoleon Bonaparte, who(m) the Spanish would soon hand over the territory to/to whom the Spanish would soon hand over the territory.

j) Any foreign power which/that controlled the Mississippi and New Orleans was a danger to the United States.

k) So Jefferson advised Robert Livingston, who was the American ambassador to France, to make an offer to buy the city of New Orleans.

l) Napoleon, whose wars in Europe were very costly, considered the offer.

m) He found out that Louisiana was a territory (which/that) he couldn't really use and (which/that) he could make a lot of money with. / He found out that Louisiana was a territory (which/that) he couldn't really use and with which he could make a lot of money.

n) So he offered the Americans the purchase of the whole of Louisiana, which, however, not all Americans favored.

o) The price (which/that) the French and the Americans finally agreed upon was $ 15 million. / The price upon which the French and the Americans finally agreed was $ 15 million. / $ 15 million was the price (which/that) the French and the Americans finally agreed upon.

p) The territory (which/that) Jefferson purchased included nearly a million square miles. / Jefferson purchased a territory which/that included nearly a million square miles.

q) The land, which thirteen states were formed from in all, cost the Americans less than four cents an acre. / The land, from which thirteen states were formed in all, cost the Americans less than four cents an acre. / In all, thirteen states were formed from this land, which cost the Americans less than four cents an acre.

Aufgabe 9* Nach der Unabhängigkeit von England umfassten die Vereinigten Staaten zunächst ein relativ kleines Gebiet vom Atlantik bis zum Mississippi. a
Mit dem Kauf von Louisiana (der *Louisiana Purchase*) wurde das Staatsgebiet plötzlich um ein Drittel größer, wobei die westliche Grenze selbst im Vertrag nicht genau bezeichnet war. b+c
Entscheidend war, dass die Vereinigten Staaten sich jetzt ungehindert nach Westen ausbreiten konnten, weil dort keine fremde Macht Territorium besaß. d
Louisiana kam 1803 zu den USA, aber kaum jemand interessierte sich für dieses weithin unbekannte und weit entfernte Land. e+f
Lediglich der Mississippi war von Bedeutung, und zwar für viele Siedler in Kentucky und Tennessee. Sie mussten ihre Farmerzeugnisse auf dem Fluss nach New Orleans bringen, wo allerdings spanische Beamte den Hafen immer wieder für amerikanische Produkte sperrten, oft von einem Tag auf den anderen und ohne jede Angabe von Gründen. g+h
Außerdem machte sich der amerikanische Präsident Jefferson Sorgen, weil die Spanier beabsichtigten, das Gebiet an Napoleon Bonaparte abzutreten; im Übrigen sahen es die Amerikaner prinzipiell als Gefahr, dass ein anderes Land den Mississippi und New Orleans kontrollierte. i+j
Der amerikanische Botschafter in Frankreich bekam von Jefferson den Auftrag, ein Angebot für den Kauf der Stadt New Orleans abzugeben. k
Napoleon, der in Europa in kostspielige Kriege verwickelt war, ging sogar noch weiter: Louisiana war für ihn ziemlich nutzlos, also bot er den Amerikanern ganz Louisiana an, denn das war für ihn einträglicher. l+m+n
Zwar waren nicht alle Amerikaner einverstanden, aber schließlich wurde man sich für 15 Millionen Dollar handelseinig. n+o
Aus den fast 1 Million Quadratkilometern wurden 13 Bundesstaaten. Das Land dafür hatte pro Morgen ($\approx 4\,000\,m^2$) weniger als 4 Cent gekostet. p+q

Indirekte Rede

ufgabe 1 a) ... is sure she'll get a good job as an apprentice.

b) Cindy says that she has always worked hard at school.

c) Cindy says that she'd like to be a bank clerk.

d) Cindy says that she wrote her fifteenth letter of application yesterday, and that she's going to write some more if she has to.

e) Cindy says that her parents have been helping her a lot.

f) Cindy says that she hopes her grandma will go on giving her money.

g) Cindy says that she'll rent a room of her own as soon as she has a job.

ufgabe 2 a) ... she would get a good job as an apprentice.

b) She said that she had always worked hard at school.

c) She said that she'd like to be a bank clerk.

d) She said that she had written her fifteenth letter of application yesterday, and that she was going to write some more if she had to.

e) She said that her parents had been helping her a lot.

f) She said that she hoped her grandma would go on giving her money.

g) She said that she'd rent a room of her own as soon as she had a job.

Aufgabe 3 On Friday, Adrian wrote that his precious love left the town (those shores) the next day. He wrote he was going to the airport to see her off. He hoped her plane wouldn't suffer from metal fatigue. He explained that he had just checked the world map to see where Tunisia is/was and that he was most relieved to see that Pandora wouldn't have to fly through the Bermuda triangle.

He wrote that if anything had happened to his love he would never have smiled again. He wrote that he had bought her a book to read during the flight; it was called *Crash!*, by a bloke called William Goldenstein, III. He added that it was very good on what to do if the worst happened.

On Saturday, Adrian wrote that Pandora had read the *Crash!* book in the coach on the way to the airport and that when her flight had been called she had had slight hysterics and her father had had to carry her up the steps. He added that he had waved to the plane until it had retreated into a large cloud, then he had sadly got on a coach and had come back home. How he would get through the next fortnight he didn't know. He bade his Tunisian beauty goodnight.

Aufgabe 4 Mathew told me that he wanted more pocket money. I asked him what he had said, and he repeated that he would like to have more pocket money. I asked him to first tell me why he wanted more, and he explained that he hadn't got enough to buy himself all the things he wanted. I wanted to know what he wanted to buy, so he replied that he didn't really know, CDs, books, and so on. I told him that I gave him fifteen pounds every month and that had to be enough. But he insisted, saying that all his classmates got much more. I asked him who got how much, and he answered that he thought Andy had got thirty pounds last month. I said that was what he thought and told him to ask Andy if he didn't really know. But he begged me to give him a little more, so I finally wondered how much I should give him. In the end I told him I would give him twenty pounds next month. I asked him if that was all right, and he answered that was great, and thanked me.

Aufgabe 5 My dad wanted to know what I was going to do that evening, so I asked him if I hadn't told him about that pop concert, and I added that I was sure it would be great. But he was surprised and said that he didn't want me to go to pop concerts when I hadn't finished my homework! So I told him that I could do my homework the next day, and then, Tim and Tom were coming, too. But he shouted that he didn't care about Tim and Tom, and told me to stop talking about them and said that I spent too much time with them. I replied that we always had a lot of fun together, but he said that fun wasn't everything. He asked me if I remembered what I had promised him and my mum after I had shown them my bad school report the year before/last year. I said alright, but I had been working all afternoon, and I would have gone on if that concert hadn't been taking place that evening. So in the end he said okay, I was allowed to go that day, but I had to do my homework the next day.

Aufgabe 6 When my father asked me last night why I was so happy all the time, I told him that I had received/had some good news. Of course he wanted to know what was going on. I told him I was going camping with seven girls and boys from my class the following weekend. I saw that he wanted to ask me why I hadn't told him before, but then he didn't ask that question but told me to pack my things for the weekend as early as possible, and he added that he could take three of us to the station in his car, so we didn't have to carry everything ourselves. Of course I didn't say no!

fgabe 7*

MOTHER 1: What can my husband and I do if we find out that our daughter has stolen something from a supermarket?

MR SMITH: Give the things back, talk to her and try to solve her problems, because she wouldn't steal if she had no problems.

MOTHER 2: What would you do if your child broke into a house?

MR SMITH: I don't really know, I hope the atmosphere in our family is good enough that my children will never become criminals.

TEACHER: You have been talking about children of 10 to 16 years. I wonder what happens to older youngsters.

MR SMITH: There are the same sentences for young offenders between 17 and 20, but more of them are sent to special prisons.

FATHER: Do you have any suggestions about how crime is best prevented?

MR SMITH: I must admit I'm afraid the only thing we can do is to show children that they don't have to have everything they see.

TEACHER: Won't the government have to do something about it if there are more and more young criminals?

MR SMITH: I agree with you, but they have done a lot already. Still, more has to be done to help families to give their children enough care and love.

MOTHER 3: I would never have thought that my 8-year-old son would steal something, but yesterday I wanted to pay at the greengrocer's and found out that twenty pounds were missing from my purse. Should I punish him, or is it enough to talk to him?

MR SMITH: You don't really have to punish him, but you should make sure that he understands what he has done, and that you understand why he did it.

ufgabe 8

a) S: Hi, Tom!

S: Hey, what's the matter? What have I done to you?

T: Oh, it's nothing. Everything alright!

S: Oh no, you can tell that to your grandmother! What has happened? Come on, tell me!

T: Well, alright. You know, our soccer team lost that important match yesterday.

S: But that isn't so terrible, is it?

T: Yes, it is, silly! Our school has been in the city finals for twelve years now, and this year we won't be there. And then, you know, it was my fault that we lost.

S: Oops. Your fault? How come?

T: Well, a few minutes before the end of the match, we still had a draw – zero all. And then I tried to kick the ball to Pete, but one of Tottenham Road's players got the ball, dribbled to the goal and scored.

S: But then it's not just your fault. The goalie should have paid attention.

T: Oh, shut up. He did pay attention, but he had no chance. I knew it: you don't know anything about soccer!

S: But Tom, don't run away! Tom! ... What an idiot!

b) "I said hello to Tom, but he didn't seem to hear me. So I asked him what the matter was and what I had done to him. Tom finally answered that it was nothing and everything was alright. But I insisted, saying he could tell that to his grandmother. I wanted to know what had happened, and I asked him to tell me. So at last he admitted that his soccer team had lost that important match yesterday. When I told him I thought that wasn't so terrible, he shouted it was. He explained our school had been in the city finals for twelve years now, and this year we wouldn't be. And then he said it was his fault that they had lost. Of course I asked him how that was possible. He explained that a few minutes before the end they had still had a draw – zero all. And then he had tried to kick the ball to Pete, but one of Tottenham Road's players had got the ball, had dribbled to the goal and had scored. I tried to cheer him up by saying that then it hadn't been just his fault: the goalie should have paid attention. But he cried that the goalie had paid attention, but he had had no chance. And then he said he had known that I didn't know anything about soccer and ran away. I shouted after him not to run away, but then I thought that he was quite an idiot."

Schwierige Aufgaben zum Knobeln

ufgabe 1

N	I	G	H	T		S	I	G	H	T	S		O
O		U		H	E	A	R		O	W		B	U
	D	E	A	R		L		F	L	O	W	E	R
N		S		E	Y	E		O	E		H		
O		S	E	W			B	R		S	E	A	
S	E	E	N		B	U	Y		B	O	R	E	D
E		D		B	L	U	E		K	N	E	W	

Across

1 which/that
4 When
8 (In order) To
10 with
11 if
14 can
15 with
17 of
18 participle
19 some
20 of
21 A
22 irregular

Down

1 say
2 puzzle
3 a/your
4 are
5 through
6 A
7 determiner
9 auxiliary
11 A
12 word
13 for
16 somebody/someone
17 not

ufgabe 2

[1]have arrived, [2]have never been, [3]was reading, [4]saw, [5]liked, [6]booked, [7]didn't want, [8]was, [9]were trying, [10]managed, [11]haven't you put, [12]haven't brought/didn't bring, [13]didn't pack, [14]couldn't, [15]didn't you ask, [16]went, [17]You heard, [18]was going, [19]didn't you, [20]were you doing, [21]left, [22]wasn't listening, [23]had taken, [24]haven't/hadn't got, [25]had tried, [26]had had to, [27]happened, [28]tried/were trying, [29]was hammering, [30]turning, [31]came, [32]ran, [33]made, [34]did, [35]hadn't even looked, [36]was, [37]lived, [38]have heard, [39]Have/Did you read, [40]gave, [41]haven't/didn't, [42]have learnt/ learned, [43]has prepared, [44]have been reading

Aufgabe 3

Do you often go to parties, Lizzy?
When are you going home, Fiona?
Where did you spend the holidays, Carol?
When was your wallet stolen, Steven?
Are you enjoying yourself, Tom?
How long have you been working at that hairdresser's now, Max?
What were you doing when I came, Linda?
Who told you about that job, Denise?

Aufgabe 4

a) … if she often went to parties, and she answered that she didn't often go to parties because she didn't really like them.

b) Berty asked Fiona when she was going home, and she answered that she was going home at ten.

c) Charly asked Carol where she had spent the holidays, and she answered that she had spent them in Italy.

d) Sandy asked Steven when his wallet had been stolen, and he answered that it had been stolen the day before.

e) Betty asked Tom if he was enjoying himself, and he answered that he was really enjoying himself.

f) Oprah asked Max how long he had been working at that hairdresser's then, and he answered that he had been working there for seven months.

g) Jennifer asked Linda what she had been doing when Jennifer had come, and Linda answered that she had been watching 'The X-Files' when Jennifer had come.

h) Harry asked Denise who had told her about that job, and she answered that her aunt had told her about it.

Aufgabe 5

[1]called, [2]born, [3]travelling/to travel, [4]hunting, [5]shooting, [6]calling/to call, [7]aiming, [8]trained, [9]to give, [10]Having entertained, [11]of starting, [12]showing/to show, [13]to make, [14]to miss, [15]seeing, [16]to imagine, [17]Being, [18]having, [19]sleeping, [20]living, [21]of being, [22]being/to be, [23]hunting, [24]to eat, [25]named, [26]to join, [27]to do, [28]to present, [29]acting, [30]playing, [31]of working, [32]wondering/to wonder, [33]to continue, [34]of being, [35]to become, [36]starting/to start, [37]to perform, [38]trying, [39]to try, [40]to create/creating, [41]touring, [42]starring, [43]known, [44]buying/having bought, [45]seeing/having seen, [46]watching, [47]of riding, [48]smelling, [49]to put, [50]advertising, [51]to come, [52]to tour

ufgabe 6 Of course, young offenders cannot be treated the same way adult criminals are treated. Children aren't sent to prison with grown-ups (although it must be said that prison was made a possibility for 12- to 14-year-olds in October 1994 (by the British government)), but sometimes a strict sentence must be passed.

Young offenders between 10 and 16 are brought before a special court. In the past, these courts were given the name 'juvenile court', but since 1992, they have been called 'youth courts'. Other details were changed (by the government) in 1992, too, but these details needn't be discussed here. Only the most important things are being talked about today. If a child is found guilty, he will be ordered to pay for the damage he has done/that has been done or he will be made to pay a fine. Another possibility is ordering that the child be supervised by a social worker for some time. For very serious crimes, however, imprisonment may be ordered in a place (which is) agreed to by the Home Secretary …

ufgabe 7

a) … (who/whom/that) people of the United States see as one of the greatest leaders in the history of their country.

b) … (which/that) many thousands of Americans visit every year.

c) Kentucky is the state (which/that) Abraham Lincoln was born in. / … the state in which Abraham Lincoln was born.

d) The family (which/that) Lincoln was born into were poor farmers. / The family into which Lincoln was born were poor farmers.

e) 1831 is the year in which Lincoln left the family farm. / … the year (which/that) Lincoln left the family farm in.

f) The other qualities (which/that) Lincoln was known for were, among others, fairness and honesty. / … qualities for which Lincoln was known were, …

g) He only defended people in court whose cases were right and just in his eyes.

h) Lincoln became President at the moment at which the nation was in its greatest crisis since 1776.

i) The independence of the 13 American colonies was the moment at which the real history of the United States began.

j) The Civil War was a war which/that was fought between the states, between fathers and sons, brothers and brothers. It was a war which/that caused terrible bloodshed and almost destroyed the nation.

k) Lincoln's most important achievement (which/that) we think of today is the end of slavery.
l) No, he couldn't. The happier life (which/that) everybody hoped for after the end of the war did not last long for Lincoln.
m) The last few hours (which/that) Lincoln spent/lived were spent in a theater in Washington, D.C.
n) His influence and importance are the things (which/that) everybody agrees upon. / … the things upon which everybody agrees.

Aufgabe 8
a) think, see
b) weren't, wouldn't visit
c) wouldn't put/wouldn't have put, hadn't done
d) had been, would perhaps have had
e) could have gone, had existed
f) wouldn't have become, hadn't worked
g) hadn't had, wouldn't be
h) will only defend, is
i) hadn't already abolished, wouldn't have happened
j) could have been, hadn't separated
k) asked, used, will have to, can be
l) would certainly have done, hadn't been
m) still existed, would have been
n) lived, wouldn't be
o) will only change, dare

Aufgabe 9
1known, 2even, 3the, 4by, 5Duck, 6Although, 7being, 8and, 9mainly, 10said, 11good, 12to, 13have, 14and, 15truly, 16force, 17making, 18have, 19The, 20it, 21was, 22in, 23of, 24to, 25where, 26the, 27scenes, 28farm, 29sold, 30the, 31he, 32business, 33his, 34lot, 35World, 36an, 37Red, 38having, 39cartoon, 40in, 41new, 42Studio, 43the, 44many, 45on, 46which, 47joined, 48story, 49actors, 50the, 51working, 52entertainment, 53give, 54nature, 55films, 56long, 57he, 58park, 59begun, 60today, 61After, 62in, 63was, 64had, 65taken, 66on, 67same, 68directly, 69his

Bildnachweis

S. 3: Archiv für Kunst und Geschichte, Berlin; S. 3: A People and a Nation. A History of the United States, Houghton Mifflin Company Boston, 1986; S. 88: Edward Dorville; S. 98: USIA; S. 104: USIA; S. 114: USIA; S. 118: A People and a Nation. A History of the United States, Houghton Mifflin Company Boston, 1986; S. 125: Chloe Musman; S. 128: A People and a Nation. A History of the United States, Houghton Mifflin Company Boston, 1986; S. 135: Robert J. Dixon & Herbert Fox: The USA, Men and History, Regents Publishing Company, Inc. 1975; S. 140: a) USIA; (1) Robert J. Dixon & Herbert Fox: The USA, Men and History, Regents Publishing Company, Inc. 1975; b) Raches L. Chapman: The USA, Men and Machines, Regents Publishing Company, Inc. 1968; (2) Werner Büdeler: Das Abenteuer der Mondlandung. Bertelsmann Sachbuchverlag Reinhard Mohn, Gütersloh, 1969; S. 141: c) Werner Büdeler: Das Abenteuer der Mondlandung. Bertelsmann Sachbuchverlag Reinhard Mohn, Gütersloh, 1969; (3) USIA; d) USIA; (5) Transglobe; f) USIA; (6) Raches L. Chapman: The USA, Men and Machines, Regents Publishing Company, Inc. 1968; S. 142: a) Robert J. Dixon & Herbert Fox: The USA, Men and History, Regents Publishing Company, Inc. 1975; c) USIA; d) www.camelotintl.com/heritage/name.html; S. 143: e) Robert J. Dixon & Herbert Fox: The USA, Men and History, Regents Publishing Company, Inc. 1975; f) Raches L. Chapman: The USA, Men and Machines, Regents Publishing Company, Inc. 1968; h) by courtesy of the National Portrait Gallery, London; S. 144: A People and a Nation. A History of the United States, Houghton Mifflin Company Boston, 1986

Ihre Meinung ist uns wichtig!

Ihre Anregungen sind uns immer willkommen. Bitte informieren Sie uns mit diesem Schein über Ihre Verbesserungsvorschläge!

Titel-Nr.	Seite	Vorschlag

Bitte hier abtrennen

Zutreffendes bitte ankreuzen!

Die Absenderin/der Absender ist:

- ☐ Lehrer/in in den Klassenstufen: ____
- ☐ Fachbetreuer/in
  Fächer: ____
- ☐ Seminarlehrer/in
  Fächer: ____
- ☐ Regierungsfachberater/in
  Fächer: ____
- ☐ Oberstufenbetreuer/in
- ☐ Schulleiter/in
- ☐ Referendar/in, Termin 2. Staats-examen: ____
- ☐ Leiter/in Lehrerbibliothek
- ☐ Leiter/in Schülerbibliothek
- ☐ Sekretariat
- ☐ Eltern
- ☐ Schüler/in, Klasse: ____
- ☐ Sonstiges: ____

Unterrichtsfächer: (Bei Lehrkräften!)

____

STARK Verlag
Postfach 1852
85318 Freising

13-V1M

Bitte ausfüllen und im frankierten Umschlag an uns einsenden. Für Fensterkuverts geeignet.

Kennen Sie Ihre Kundennummer?
Bitte hier eintragen.

Absender (Bitte in Druckbuchstaben!)

Name/Vorname ____

Straße/Nr. ____

PLZ/Ort ____

Telefon privat ____ Geburtsjahr ____

E-Mail-Adresse ____

Schule/Schulstempel (Bitte immer angeben!)

Bitte hier abtrennen

(Bitte blättern Sie um)